Take Back Your Light

A Lightworker's Guide to Balance, Clearing, and Protection

Heather Robinson

Dear Corey,
Shine bright!
Heather

Take Back your Light:
A Lightworker's Guide to Balance, Clearing, and Protection

ISBN: 978-1-7359730-0-5

Front cover image by Luizclas on Pexels.com @Luisclaz
Cover design by Heather Robinson
Interior design by Heather Robinson

First printing edition 2020

www.heatherhealingarts.com

This book is dedicated to my children,
Hannah and Ethan. May you always remember
to shine your own unique light.

CONTENTS

CONTENTS

Foreword

Another title for this book might have been "Stumbling Toward Enlightenment." It began writing itself about two decades ago in 2000 when, in hindsight, I can clearly see I was being called into service as a lightworker. Twenty years have flown by as I have tripped and skipped down the path toward enlightenment while becoming comfortable my own flavor of spirituality that is well with my soul.

Spirituality. There it is. That word makes some people turn up their noses and cross my name off their friend list with a big black Sharpie marker of judgment! That's okay. This book may not be for you just yet. Spirituality for me is the belief that there is something greater than myself that connects me to every living thing on this planet. For me that something greater is God. I'll respect your choice to experience God however you choose regardless of whatever name, religion, or doctrine God is for you. For me God is The Light.

In 2009 I was participating in a class at my church called Alpha© - An Exploration of Christian Faith. That 12-week course profoundly changed my life and afterwards, I continued to help lead the program for the next four years. I have been raised in the Presbyterian church, and also the Baptist and Methodist churches too depending on which house I woke up in on Sunday morning - my Dad's, Mom's, or Grandparents'. Faith wasn't a new thing to me, but the understanding of a loving, mature relationship with the Divine was a new idea for me to wrap my head around. It was during this season of praying with others, exploring how God and angels work in our daily lives, and leaning on my higher power for strength that I felt my spiritual gifts develop more rapidly. A true season of enlightenment.

Along this journey I have committed myself to be guided by the Light. I have felt the Light as I sang hymns of praise in the antique pews of my humble North Carolina home church. I have been in awe of the Light as I stood in the Vatican and gazed upward at the ceiling of the Sistine Chapel and Michelangelo's glorious painting "The Last Judgment." I have touched the Light as I held a sick child so her mother could breastfeed her brother in a sweltering clinic in Blanchard, Haiti. I have been moved by the Light as I joined in ancient Native American songs of prayer with friends that became family in a Lakota inipi (sweat lodge).

In Alpha© I learned that when you step into the light, when you commit to a daily walk with God, the darkness will try to extinguish your light. In my experience that has been profoundly true! I am by nature a nurturer and a helper. My intent with this book is to share with you my experiences which have led to this collection of spiritual tools to help you push back the darkness, take back your own precious light, and stand in your truth.

Through the years I have been blessed with many amazing teachers and guides who helped to form my belief base and fill my toolbox with priceless metaphysical tools which I have shared here with you in this book. I am in such gratitude to them all and did my best to give credit where credit is due. They have helped me to learn many of the methods and tools described in this book. Each of these tools will help you balance, clear, and protect your light. This lightworker's guide is a collection of my healing arts tools that I frequently share with my clients, friends, and family when they ask for my guidance. I have tried them all! They really work and I am thrilled to share them with you.

Author Barbara Taylor Brown states, "I have learned things in the dark that I could never have learned in the light, things that have saved my life over and over again, so that there is really only one logical conclusion. I need darkness as much as I need light." This book was born out of many dark days and dark nights of the soul. Challenging times and missteps that have enabled me to share this guidebook with you. Creating it was a labor of love inspired by the Light. I hope that it brings you both entertainment and enlightenment. I pray that it encourages you to step out and take back your light!

- Heather Robinson, Lightworker

A Brief Note About 2020: The Year Our Light Went Out

2020 began as a normal year, didn't it? Remember New Year's Eve and the excitement of a new decade? Well that hopeful fantasy quickly took a turn to negative town! 2020 arrived as a typical year and then the COVID-19 global pandemic, the CoronaVirus, rocked the whole world. It completely bombed everyone's root chakra. The root chakra deals with issues of safety, fear, stability, home, family, security, abundance and lack, health and illness. In one fail swoop, all of humanity took a gut punch dead center in all those emotional topics. When bad things happen, when the darkness settles over your life, your light goes out and it can be incredibly difficult to get it back.

Suddenly we were forced to close our businesses and shelter in place while we scrambled to prepare for battle against an invisible enemy the CoronaVirus. Within a matter of days we were forced into lock down where we were supposed to quickly transition our jobs to be able to work from home while simultaneously homeschooling our panicked children. We were forced to social distance from elderly parents and family who needed our care. We had to cancel weddings and reunions, skip holidays and family gatherings. We succumbed to the chaos of hoarding toilet paper and hand sanitizer! We were programmed to fear anyone who wasn't wearing a face mask and were told that we would catch virus if we stood less than six feet from another person. Frightened pregnant mothers had to labor and deliver alone, struggling under face masks anxious about the dystopian world their baby was being born into. Hospitalized COVID patients suffered and died alone quarantined apart from loved ones. While every day the mass media shoved the death tolls at us along with new dramas like mandatory face masks, city-wide curfews, mandatory stay-at-home orders, violent race riots, economic collapse, virtual learning, and other enormous reductions in our personal freedoms.

Add these emotional triggers to our already extensive list of modern stressors - debt, health, job loss, relationship issues, loss of a loved one, Internet bullies, world events - and the result is an acute increase in depression, mental health issues, suicide, domestic violence and trauma. That is an enormous amount of darkness to overcome for a global population who have lost their light.

What's coming next? As I write this it's only August of 2020 and I can't even fathom what other obscurities we face in coming months. Despite all this uncertainty and constant change I have faith that we are capable of shifting to survive. It's time to step out of the darkness. Gather round my little firecrackers, it's time for you to own your power and take back your light. This book is written especially for you! - Heather

CHAPTER 1

What is your light?

Illuminating the Unique You. Shine on!

Let it shine!

Your light is the life force inside you. It's your magnetic personality. It's your peace and radiance. It's the life force that attracts people to you. Your light is the hope that diminishes dread. It is the positive that overrides the negative. It is your protective armor. It is your unwavering faith when the world seeks to crush your will. It is your pure energy. It is pure love. It is your soul. It is the spark of the Holy Spirit, God, the Divine within you It is your true self and it is time for you to let it shine!

What does your light look like?

Think of your light as a light bulb or a flame. Imagine it looks like the sun or a lighthouse. It glows from the center of your body and reaches out in all directions from your core. When your mood is low or when you are afraid, stressed, angry, or anxious it dims your light. When you are emotionally balanced and peaceful your light shines bright. Your light will be extinguished when you feel persecuted, oppressed, abused, or manipulated. When you own your power, speak your truth and courageously lead with love your light will turn up to supernova and shine brightly.

Where is your light?

Your light lives in your chakras. Chakras are energy centers located throughout your body and are the keys to your physical and emotional health. When your chakras are in balance your light shines bright. There are seven main chakras in the body (and 114 overall). Imagine that each chakra is the size of an 8"-10" plate that extends in front of and behind your body as spinning centers of energy.

The Seven Chakras

Crown: I trust
I know. I understand.

Connection to the Divine, living in the now, spirituality, self knowledge, peace

Third Eye: I see
...and it is safe to see.
I let go of control.

Insight, intuition, truth, vision, inspiration, "knowing" that is beyond words

Throat: I speak
I speak my truth.
I listen.

Communication, listening, issues of timing, manifestation, integrity

Heart: I Love
It is safe to love.
I give and receive.

Compassion, personal freedom, surrender, forgiveness, acceptance, gateway to higher self, relationships, balance

Solar Plexus: I will
I have power. I think. I act.

Power, self esteem, courage, synthesis of ideas and feelings, judgments, ego, energy, fear

Sacral (Belly): I feel
I believe in myself. I want.

Emotional & sexual issues, attachment and letting go, body image, creativity, pleasure, motivation, desire

Root: I am
I am safe. I have. I live.

Survival issues, anger, passion, lust, money, career, shelter, pain, safety, issues of abundance vs. lack, grounding

What dims your light?

Toxic people, energy vampires, prolonged stressful situations can all dim your light. Sometimes we cling to difficult times and difficult people even though they are trying to be removed from our lives. When you're upset or hold on to emotional wounds or past traumas, your chakras become sluggish and blocked. Trapped emotions stagnate your chakras and cut your power. This results in physical ailments, emotional distress, sickness - all of which are general dis-ease. It's crucial to keep your chakras in balance for your optimal health and to keep your light shining bright!

How to ignite your light

First you need to calm your mind and feel centered. Centered is a term used to describe returning to a feeling of emotional balance. Activities such as yoga, exercise, napping, breathing techniques help you feel more calm and centered. Engaging in things that bring you joy center you too - like singing, dancing, cooking, painting, or laughing. When you're bombarded by negative energy your chaotic "monkey mind" can take over throwing you off center and making it difficult to maintain your light.

CHAPTER 2

Quiet Your Monkey Mind

6 Groovy Tools to Rekindle Your Light

Do you spend your life rushing from one thing to the next, managing crisis after crisis, constantly worrying about things you can't control? Odds are you are living with a monkey mind. Imagine you're in the jungle surrounded by dozens of wild, screaming monkeys that are swinging from tree to tree. Now imagine those monkeys are inside your mind howling for your attention. That mental jungle is "monkey mind." Monkey mind is a Buddhist metaphor that describes the natural state of our chaotic mind. Monkey mind feeds on stimuli, so when you feed it too much info or too many decisions at once it goes wild! If you are overwhelmed your monkey mind can take over.

Your negative thoughts, fears and self-doubt often scream at you louder than logical thoughts. The loudest monkey of them all is the one that represents the fears of your inner child. Hurts and hang-ups from long ago can taunt your mind with comments like:

"No one will ever love you."
"You sound so stupid."
"Don't even try. You're going to fail."
"You aren't smart enough."
"All of this is your fault."

Monkey mind is the worst! When you can't find your way out of the mental jungle there is no way your light can stay on. These healing tools will help you quiet your monkey mind and get back your peace and clarity. Use these tools any time you feel off balance.

Detox your body

Sugar, alcohol, caffeine, fast food, processed food, fried food, nicotine, vape pens, flour, genetically modified grains - you've heard this list before and you know these things are bad for you. It's time to remove them because they are snuffing out your precious light. Any addictive substances are toxic for your sensitive body. While they provide a temporary high, they are contributing to your mood swings and anxiety, as well as wrecking your internal organs. I'm not saying it is going to be easy, but I am saying it will be worth it! Also, focusing on healthy nutrition amps your intuition.

Meditation

Meditation is a great way to quiet the monkey mind, balance your chakras and amp up your light. It does take practice and patience, so as a beginner give yourself a lot. Start by trying to hold your focus for two to three minutes and work up to ten minutes. For newbies it helps to focus on a visual in your mind like a serene lake, a babbling brook, or ocean waves gently rolling onto shore. Even short periods of meditation are super helpful and the results are so worth it.

Some proven benefits of meditation include: lower blood pressure, improved blood circulation, lower heart rate, slower respiratory rate, less anxiety, lower cortisol levels, increased feelings of well-being, less stress, and deeper relaxation - all of which ignite your light!

Ground yourself

Grounding is a quick and simple tool to reclaim your energy and can be done inside or out. It helps you refocus by reconnecting your body to the ground. Literally just your shoes off and put your feet on Mother Earth! If the weather doesn't permit, just put your bare feet on the floor. Spread out your toes to get a steady "grip." Gently rock back and forth through the heels and balls of your feet. Don't lock out your knees. Relax your arms, neck, jaw, and shoulders. Close your eyes, take deep breaths and imagine the stress and negativity flowing out of your body, from head to foot, out through your feet and into the earth. You can also sit on the ground, lie down on the ground, or sit in a chair with your feet on the earth. Ahh! It's just that simple.

Remember to play

What makes you happy? What makes your heart sing? Go do THAT! Whatever gets your creative juices flowing is a joyful way to ignite your inner light! Turn on some happy music, pick a coloring book, grab some crayons, colored pencils or juicy markers and invite your inner child to sit with you awhile in a peaceful, creative fun activity. Coloring is not your jam? Try painting, pottery, sewing, needlepoint, knitting, dancing, playing music, go for a run or jump rope - just have fun.

"But I'm not creative," you say. Nonsense! Rock what you've got and silence that inner critic. Set your soul on fire with activities that get you moving! Ones that spark joy in your heart, make you laugh, and make you happy.

Practice mindfulness

Mindfulness is the awareness of "some-thing" while meditation is the awareness of "no-thing." You can apply mindfulness throughout your day. No kidding! Practice mindfulness while you fold laundry or walk the dog. The goal is to focus your mind on one activity. Mindfulness is the opposite of multitasking! Running, mowing the lawn, rocking your infant are all mindful activities. They are moving meditations! Focus on the rhythm of your body and your breath and totally remain in the present moment. Feel your body as it moves through the activity and be grateful for this moment of time.

Take a dip

If your zodiac sign is Cancer, Pisces, Scorpio (water signs) this should be your go-to peace-out activity. Dive into the ocean, a lake, a river, pool, or simply take a long soak in a warm bathtub of Epsom Salt.

Magnesium and sulfate are the two main ingredients in Epsom Salt. Magnesium is a natural mineral your body needs to function. Healthy magnesium levels promote the production of melatonin, which supports quality sleep. Sulfate helps strengthen the digestive tract organs. This combo helps the body in releasing toxins. A warm Epsom Salt bath is a simple, self-care healing tool you can treat yourself to everyday.

Our deepest fear is not
that we are inadequate.
Our deepest fear is
that we are powerful
beyond measure.

It is our Light, not our
Darkness, that most
frightens us. - Marianne Williamson

CHAPTER 3

Modern Problems that Drain Your Light

People, Places and Things that Totally Wreck Your Vibe

You might have chosen this book as you were searching for some woo-woo methods to help you raise your vibration and shine your light. We will get to those! They are all here; but first things first. Let's discuss some pertinent modern problems that threaten and drain your light every day. These are all so common, you probably don't even factor them in to why you feel bad, why your mood is a mess or why your six-sensory skills aren't working so well anymore.

Have you ever walked into a place and thought "Wow, it feels really weird in here," or "This place has a really negative vibe!" There's a good chance the space had a residual negative energy and needs to be cleared. Remember, light is energy and energy is light. Positive or negative energy affects not only your body, but also the spaces and places where you live, work, and play.

Every day you are bombarded with negative energy and toxic people. Energy or emotional vampires feed off you in person and on social media. You are inundated with frightening news stories and angry social media posts. It is so easy to absorb or take on these lower energies without realizing the effect that it has on your mood, health and overall well-being and how it can seriously diminish your light. Here are some common, modern problems that suck your light every day and how to combat the drainage so you can vibe higher.

Energy Vampires: Stop sucking my light!

Energy Vampire, Downer, Fun Sucker are a few slang terms for toxic people who feed off your energy. Who are they? They can be a co-worker, a friend, or a family member. The vampire might even be you! Toxic people can knowingly or unknowingly drain your light when they are depressed, manipulative, gossipy, jealous, vindictive, narcissistic, or just down right mean.

If your energy or immune system is low, you can easily fall prey to an energy vampire. If they have low self esteem or feel powerless, they will draw from your light to boost their energy, leaving you depleted. Smudging, crystals, psychic protection shields, and affirmations can protect you from the vamps. We will discuss those protection tools in the following chapters. But first, take inventory of the folks in your life. Do they uplift you or leave you drained? If someone is not empowering you, then they are draining you. You may have heard about raising your vibration - your vibe attracts your tribe! Well, your high vibe also attracts folks who want to charge their battery off your juice! Toxic people destroy your light and they've got to go!

Clutter

Your light can't shine if it's buried among mounds of old magazines, piles of clothes you haven't worn in decades, and cabinets full of mismatched Tupperware. Often your physical clutter is a reflection of your emotional overload. Empaths tend to have more physical clutter because they are too busy running around caring for the needs of everyone else to manage their own space. Ignoring clutter in your space and in your soul can lead to continued self sabotage. Your physical clutter can help you see other areas of your life that need attention: your relationships, your ego, your finances, etc. The good news is it can be cleared!

"Tidying (releasing clutter) orders and relaxes the mind."
- Marie Kondo

Kerri Richardson, lifestyle designer and author of the best selling book "What Your Clutter is Trying to Tell You" says that physical clutter is a reflection of emotional clutter. She notes there are three common causes of clutter:

- unrealistic expectations.
- limiting beliefs.
- the need for boundaries.

One or all of these three issues may be draining your light right now and preventing you from living your best life. Things have energy too. Take a closer look at the things you just can't seem to get rid of. What does holding on it represent for you? Have you been putting off a big clean up or a big purge? Telling yourself you'll get out there and clean the garage as soon as you have time will energetically ensure that your schedule will always be too full to do it because subconsciously you are avoiding going through the "stuff" of your life and taking action to change it. Telling yourself "I just don't have time to deal with it" sets the intention that no, you won't have time to do it! Instead

What you think, you become.
What you feel, you attract.
What you imagine, you create. - Buddha

try saying "I will feel so much better when that chore is done. I will be so much lighter when my physical space is clean."

When you address your clutter you take back your light. When you bring order to your physical space it brings peace to your soul. Your light can't shine under that stack of unopened mail or beneath those boxes of junk you bought off Home Shopping Network the last time you felt unhappy.

Each month on the full moon is a great time to release excess and unwanted clutter. Every two weeks, make a sweep of your home or office and release what no longer serves your highest good. This is the kicker...your highest good right *now*. Not your highest good when you wore a size 4 and now you're a size 10. Keep what resonates with who you really are in the present. Not the you that you were before that time that total wrecked your life. Keep what reflects the you that you are today.

Give it away, donate it, recycle it, or trash it. Heck, burn it if you want it. If you find yourself thinking that you will hold on to it until you have time to sell it, consider that time is money? Do you really have extra time to manage the sale of that thing, or are you just postponing letting it go because you're still emotionally attached to it? Believe me, I understand! As an artist I have a tough time letting go of even the smallest art supply. I've learned that holding on to it makes me hopeful for a time that I will be less busy and can be crafty once again. Simultaneously it reminds me of a happy time when I was a young mother, a stay-at-home-mom, and had the flexibility in my days to explore my creative side for myself and with my kids. My Rubbermaid bins of craft supplies remind me of the young me that was really happy and hopeful for the future. Holding on to all that stuff prevents me from stepping into the future and embracing the me I am today. So little by little, I whittle down my craft stash and release my unrealistic expectations that I can recreate that special time in my life.

Releasing clutter can be hard, but it is so worth the effort. When your space is jam packed to the rafters, there is no room for positive abundance to flow into your life like job opportunities, additional income, great new relationships, and the time to enjoy them all. Clearing up space on your counter tops, in your closet, in your attic, and garage means you can free up your light for more positive energy to shine through.

Items with emotional triggers

While we are on the subject of releasing clutter let's consider items with an emotional trigger. There may be things in your home that remind you of the past that you need to let go. If you're recovering from heartbreak, divorce, or job loss this simple and effective activity should be your top priority in reclaiming your light. You may love sleeping in that soft, XXL t-shirt from your ex lover, but if each time you wear it you are reminded of the heartache it has to go. If an item triggers a negative memory or a past hurt, get rid of it!

Photographs, jewelry, clothing, home decor - if the things in your personal space cause you even a moment of angst it is time for you to get them out of your sight. Marie Kondo also says "There are two reasons we can't let go: an attachment to the past or a fear for the future." Well, your light is going out in the present so pack that stuff up from the past and get it out of there.

Technology overload

Most of us spend our days with our eyes glued to tv, phone or computer screens. You are bombarded by messages and images, emails, texts, photos, social media posts, pop-up ads, online games, scrolling news reports, print media, radio, and TV ads. What about all the subliminal messages behind the video images? All this info overwhelms your mind, creates anxiety and drains your light. It's crucial that you unplug!

You can also reduce your exposure to mental clutter by unsubscribing from promotional emails, "unfollowing" or blocking folks on social media who make you mad, jealous, sad, or irritated in any way. Set additional filters on your social media accounts to limit the number of posts you receive each day. When all that is done, simply get off the screens! Put down the phone. Turn off the computer or TV and unplug.

A picture is worth a thousand hurts

If you see someone's photo on your phone and it makes you upset, it is time to delete them. If you can't bear to permanently delete special photos, use Google Drive, Dropbox or other cloud base storage to back-

up your pictures. "Unfollow" that person's social media account. Delete their emails in your inbox. If you have to interact or co-parent with that person, set up an email folder and apply filters so incoming emails go to the folder and don't pop up in your feed. Pack away their belongings or photos of them in your home and office and most importantly stop looking at their websites and social media accounts. If you've already physically separated yourself from the person or situation, next, disentangle your spiritual body from theirs by using the Unhooking method in Chapter 10.

Electromagnetic Field Radiation

Electromagnetic fields (EMFs) are invisible to the naked eye. Power lines, cell phone towers, computers, cell phones, tablets, Wi-Fi, routers, microwaves, fitness tracking devices, televisions, x-ray machines, and body scanners all emit electromagnetic fields or EMFs. Scientific studies with lab animals exposed to EMFs have shown certain types of cancer and other health threats including neuropsychiatric effects, cellular DNA damage, and endocrine changes. Long-term exposure to EMFs can lower your immune response and allow for increased exposure to negative energy.

Symptoms of excessive EMF exposure can include: weakened immune system, blurred vision, fatigue, memory loss, lack of focus and decreased attention span, headaches, depression, anxiety, irritability, insomnia, joint and muscle pain. Himalayan salt lamps are a great tool for reducing harmful EMFs!

Himalayan Salt Lamps are a great tool for you protecting against EMFs. They work just as well even if you don't plug them in!

6 Tips to Reduce EMF (Electromagnetic Field Radiation) Exposure

1. Turn off Wireless Functions whenever possible on your devices (routers, printers, cellphones, tablets, and laptops.) Turn off your Wi-Fi and router at night while you sleep.

2. Use Wired Devices: Revert to wired devices instead of a wireless keyboard, mouse, Bluetooth stereo speaker.

3. Keep EMF Sources at a Distance: Create distance between you and the EMF source to significantly reduce exposure levels. Cell phones give out radiation even when not in use. DO NOT: sleep with your cell phone on your nightstand or beside your head on the bed. Don't carry your cell phone in your pocket. Don't stand in front of a microwave when it is operating. Don't put your laptop computer or tablet on your lap. Move your Wi-Fi router away from where people spend the most time.

4. Keep your cellphone as far away from your body as possible. Use speakerphone features to avoid putting the phone up to your head. This is particularly important for children who are more susceptible to cell phone radiation. Look for a cellphone with a lower Specific Absorption Rate (SAR) rating.

5. Technology-Free Sleeping Areas: You (your kids) sleep 6-12 hours a day. That's a lot of consistent EMF exposure! Remove all wireless devices from the sleeping area. At night, turn your Wi-Fi cellphones, laptops, Bluetooth headsets, tablets or put them on airplane mode. Most cell phones will still work as an alarm clock in airplane mode.

6. Use crystals to deflect EMFs: Carry or wear protective crystals to block EMFs. Put them stones between you and the device in use or directly on the device. Green Aventurine is great for neutralizing all sources of EMFs from your computer, cellphone, television, Wi-Fi , etc. Some are EMF blocking crystals: amethyst, clear quartz, fluorite, black tourmaline, smoky quartz, and shungite.

CHAPTER 4

When to Clear Your Energy

"Ugh! I feel so drained!"

Energy can leave a positive or negative memory or imprint on spaces or objects like furniture, jewelry, or artwork. When you come in contact with negative energy imprints it can make you feel sick, confused, lethargic, angry or sad, and you may not understand why. If you have an uncharacteristic mood shift or physical pain when you enter a new space, or come in contact with people or new objects, tune into your light. You may need to clear your energy of negative influences. It is important to regularly clear yourself and your personal space. If you are an empath, you will likely attract more negativity than you realize and should clear and bless your surroundings more often. Remaining in contact with negative energy can seriously drain your light and put you at risk for psychic attack.

Clear your personal energy when:

- you feel physically or emotionally unwell.
- you energetically feel "off," particularly after being in contact with a toxic person
- you feel sad, depressed, overwhelmed, or have an erratic change of mood.
- you've been in an argument or hostile interaction.
- you are nervous about an upcoming confrontation.
- you feel unfocused, scattered, lethargic.
- you've had a bad day, week, or month!

Incense is a great tool for clearing your energy. It has been used in various religions for centuries. Burning incense may serve as an aid in prayer, as a means to eliminate negative energy or to dispel earthbound spirits (ghosts).

When to Clear Your Space, Home, or Office

- When the spaces just feels bad or "off"
- Before you market your home for sale.
- Before you move into a new home or work place.
- After an emotionally difficult time such as a divorce, break-up, death, illness.
- When you launch your new business in an office space and want to renew the space with purposeful and powerful intention.
- If your space has an unusual and constant feeling of gloom, dread, depression.
- If the space has a history of tragedy, illness or bad luck.
- When the people in the home/space suffer from low energy, depression, anxiety, or emotional outburts.
- When a roommate or family member moves in or out.
- If you think your space is being shared with an earthbound spirit or dark entity.
- When your space needs a fresh boost of energy like Spring cleaning.

CHAPTER 5

Smudging

The Ancient Art of Clearing, Blessing, and Protecting

Have you experienced an intense emotional upset, illness, or been in heated arguments? Does your space just feel "off?" It's time to cleanse and balance yourself and your space with sage and other smudging tools.

Smudging, or sometimes called saging, has been used by cultures around the world for thousands of years. Smudging is burning grasses or incense in ceremony or prayer in order to cleanse the body and space of impurities and connect to the spirit world. This ancient practice allows the smoke to cleanse your body or space from negativity, and to restore balance and calm. Some scientific research has shown it even kills germs! Smudging can also be used for healing, protection, purification, spiritual strength, psychic abilities, courage, connecting with your authentic self, and to release emotional pain.

Dried grasses like white sage, cedar, and sweetgrass leaves are commonly used in Native American rituals and are considered sacred holy herbs. The leaves are formed into a bundle, or smudge stick, or used in loose form and burned in a heatproof vessel such as an abalone shell or you can use any fireproof bowl.

Palo Santo wood sticks are another smudging tool that many like for its sweet smell. Palo Santo means "holy wood" in Spanish and comes from Central and South America. Palo Santo sticks leave behind less ash and aren't as messy as sage bundles.

Frankincense is a particularly powerful, ancient cleansing tool. It is derived from the resin of the Boswellia tree in the dry, mountainous regions of India, Africa and the Middle East. It is highly valued in many cultures and is known as "liquid gold," "the king of oils," and "the transformer." Frankin-

You can use an Abalone shell and loose sage to smudge.

Smudging mantra:
"I clear myself and this space of all negative energy.
I replace the darkness and heaviness with light and love."

cense has renowned healing properties for detoxing your organs/body, emotional support, and a myriad of physical ailments. It is also used to absorb negative energy, provide spiritual protection and enlightenment.

You can put a few drops of frankincense essential oil in an oil diffuser to help clear a space. Add a few drops of the oil to your sage bundle before smudging, or anoint your third eye (brow chakra) with oil before prayer, meditation or ceremony. Frankincense can also be burned as incense sticks or resin chips.

Sage, Palo Santo, incense, and frankincense oils have become mainstream! Now you can find these tools at your local metaphysical shop, at an online store, and often at local retail stores like TJ Maxx, Target, and World Market.

Setting an intention

Smudging is all about setting your intention and belief. It is simple and it gets easier with practice. An intention is a clear and positive affirmation of an outcome you want to have or experience. An intention is a statement that sets the framework for a vision or a goal of what to achieve. It begins with a mental image of the outcome you want and is fueled by faith and positive energy to help you manifest. When you intend for the person or the space to be cleared and own your power to make it so, it will be. Don't worry. You can't do it wrong. Once you get the hang of it, you will create your own intention or mantra to use when you smudge. Until then, here are some you can try!

"Bless this house, may peace dwell within.
Protect all that enter.
Bless every door, window, ceiling and wall.
Bless each room, closet, basement, Bless it all!
Bless the roof and ground surrounding with protective love and light."

"I am free of all lower energies. I raise my vibration and am surrounded by love and light."
"I banish all evil influences from myself and from this home."

"Into this smoke, I release all energies that no longer serve me, all negativity that surrounds me, and all fears that limit me. I am restored in balance and white light [of Christ]."

Frequently asked questions

- **How much do I use?** If you're using loose sage, there's no need to use the entire bundle. A leaf per room should do the trick. If you're burning a sage stick, you can snuff out the unused portion.
- **Do I have to open the windows?** Yes, sage smoke removes all the energy and it needs to escape the space.
- **Is there something I can burn for added spiritual protection?** After burning sage, you can burn rosemary to call in your ancestors for guidance and protection.
- **What if I do it wrong?** It's all about intention and belief. It's simply gets easier with practice. You can't do it incorrectly if you set your intention to clear away the dark and restore the light.

How often do I need to smudge?

Whenever the energy in your space starts to feel a little stagnant or when you feel down or negative. For some people it might be everyday, once a week, for others every month, and for others every six months. I was doing it every couple of days because I lived in a "haunted house" and it helped to keep the spirit there less active. Also if a room has residual negative or traumatic energy, you will want to clear it more often. Don't forget the corners.

CHAPTER 6

Sage Wisdom

How to Smudge Yourself and Your Surroundings

- Open a window or door or step outside into the fresh air.
- Place the sage stick, loose sage, Palo Santo, resin or incense onto a small plate, abalone shell or other heat proof vessel that will catch ashes. You can even place an incense stick in a bowl or cup of rice!
- Light the sage or other smudging tool for 30 seconds. It can take a few minutes to catch fire. Gently blow it out so it can smolder and smoke.
- Holding the smoking sage in one hand, use your other hand to waft the smoke all over your body. Begin at the top of your head, pull the smoke towards the body, coating it with smoke as you work your way down your entire body. Let the smoke cover your head, then neck and arms, then chest and torso, hips and legs, then lift each leg to allow the smoke to cover the bottom of each foot.
- As you move the smoke across your body, state your intention aloud or in your mind, *"I release all negativity from me. I am restored in balance and white light."*
- Next, wave your hand over the smoke to bring it into your stomach area, then heart, then over your head and down the back of your head. Wave your hand through the smoke three times over each body area and state aloud as you move up your body - over your stomach: "I am right acting." Heart: "I am right feeling." Head: "I am right thinking."
- Extinguish your sage bundle by rubbing it on concrete or dirt, or snuff it out on the bottom of your fireproof vessel. If there is any ash, return it to Mother Earth on the ground or flush down the toilet. Do not extinguish your smudge sticks with water! You won't be able to use them again.
- Close the window or door. Notice any subtle change in your mood and energy.
- Repeat as often as you need to eliminate low mood, anxiety, or overall funk. Practice often if you are in contact with an energy vampire or feel you have encountered paranormal or dark energy.

Step by Step Guide to Smudging Your Space & Home:

- Begin with the previous steps to smudge yourself.
- Next, open all doors and windows, even if just a crack, so the negative energy can leave the space.
- Start with the farthest room and finish at the entrance so that you push the negative energy out the front door. Holding the sage stick or smoking vessel, walk around the room allowing the smoke to fill the room. Present the smoke to each corner, the ceiling, along the walls. Be sure to smudge inside the closets, cabinets and drawers.
- Fan the smoke with your hand or a feather disperse the smoke throughout the space. Go room to room giving extra attention to areas where negative people sleep and live, where there were arguments, or where the energy feels dark, heavy or sad. As you move through the space, state your prayer or intention aloud and imagine the negativity being pushed out. A simple intention you can use is: "I clear and release all negativity from this space. I banish all darkness, heaviness, and dis-ease. This space is now filled and renewed with white light."
- Finish by the front door, smudging around the door and frame while waving the smoke out the front door. Extinguish the smudging tool as noted before. Close all the windows and doors.

CHAPTER 7

Energy Clearing Toolbox

Tips and Tools You Need to Light Up Your Vibe

Energy clearing sprays

If you're sensitive to smoke or are in a no-smoking zone like an office, you can use an energy cleansing mist instead. Fill an amber or blue glass spray bottle with half spring water and half witch hazel. Add a few drops essential oils (see chart for more info). Use 10 to 15 drops of an essential oil (1 to 3 different oils) per ounce of water. Shake well to activate the essential oil and use the spray as you would the smoking sage. You can enhance the cleansing spray by adding raw crystals such as rose quartz, citrine, or amethyst to infuse their additional healing properties.

Florida Water

Murray & Lanman's Florida Water Cologne® has both spiritual and practical purposes. Use it to attract good luck and to provide protection. Mist yourself or your space to repel negative energy and negative spirits. For high anxiety it can be applied to the forehead, back of neck, or over the solar plexus. Wipe your hands and back of neck with it when you leave any place that has intense energy to disconnect from the chaos. Florida Water is typically sold in 7.5 oz. and 2.0 oz plastic bottles. You can purchase it online or at a metaphysical shop. You may also find it at select drug stores.

Sea salt

Negative energies can leave an imprint on a room, a building or an object as a result of a tragic event. Acts of violence, heartache, sickness, death, or negative thoughts or emotions can cling to places and things. These lower energies can enter your personal space when you bring in second-hand objects like antiques, clothing, books or

Just a Dash of Salt

In 2011 I worked in a large corporate office with co-workers who were really great people - very kind and generally happy. Everyone worked really hard and the stakes were high for the projects we were trying to win, but despite the heavy workloads and pressure, it was typically a really happy work environment. As our company grew, our office expanded into a new area of the building that had previously not been inhabited. Shortly after that everyone's mood shifted.

I noticed that my co-workers continued to be moody and snarky. The entire mood of the office was really dark and sometimes confrontational. Nothing had changed about our corporate structure or workload, only the fact that we moved into a different office space. I sensed that there was a dark energy in our office. Not necessarily an earthbound spirit or ghost, but just an overall malaise and bad feelings that seemed to be affecting everyone.

Since it was a corporate office building I knew that I couldn't come in with my sage bundle and smudge the place even without setting off the fire alarms and causing my co-workers to question that earthy smell coming from my office. So instead I researched how to clear a space with tools other than sage. I discovered that you can use sea salt to clear the energy in a room or building.

One evening I stayed at the office after everyone else left. I filled 3 oz. Dixie® Cups with sea salt and hid them throughout the office building. In my boss's office, I put a cup behind an 8" x 10" picture frame of his family. I put another one behind his printer and another inside a huge potted. In the copy room, I placed a cup of sea salt behind stacks of copier paper. In the break room I put one between the refrigerator and the wall. In the conference room I hid one in the credenza behind the office supplies. Throughout the whole office I stashed away Dixie® Cups with salt and no one was the wiser.

Within 48 hours the mood in the office had lightened. Everyone in my company was on a positive uptick. So I changed out the salt every two days for about a month. After everyone had left the office, I would go around with a trash bag, dump the used sea salt into the bag and refill the cups with fresh salt. I made sure to take the trash bag out of the office and put it in the dumpster so that negative energy soaked salt was totally out of our work environment. After the month I could tell an enormous difference in the morale and the overall feeling and energy and mood of my office and of all my co-workers.

You can use sea salt at your house if someone is asthmatic or has allergies and you don't want to smudge. Fill a 3 oz. Dixie® Cup halfway with sea salt. Any brand of sea salt will work. If you don't have a paper cup you can use a coffee cup, a juice glass, a shot glass, or whatever works for you. Just make sure to go back everyday or every other day, dump the salt and replace it with fresh sea salt. Also be sure to dispose of the used salt either outside away from your house or flush it down the toilet.

You can use pink, Himalayan salt or regular sea salt to clear the energy in a home or office.

furniture from consignment or thrift stores, or hand-me-down items from your family or others. Inanimate objects can hold onto the moods and experiences of their former owners such as anger, jealousy, depression, or anxiety. If the former owner's experiences were negative or chaotic, bringing these objects in your personal space can cause you to take on those unwanted emotions.

Regardless of where negative energies originate, cleansing your space and objects from others can restore harmony and balance and break any darkness attached to them. Before you bring an antique into your home, cover and rub the furniture or artwork with dry sea salt, available at most grocery stores. Sweep off the excess salt and leave it outside. Sprinkle sea salt over your fabric furniture, bed, carpet or even on clothes worn by others, especially people who have suffered from diseases. Vacuum or sweep it up after a few hours. For jewelry, allow it to soak in a glass of sea salt for 24 hours. Dump the used salt outside or in the trash. Dispose of the trash bag away from your home. Clothing, books or furniture from consignment or thrift stores, or hand-me-down items from your family or others.

Sound healing and clearing

Prayers: Spoken prayer, mantras, songs or intentions are powerful tools to wash away negative energy. Walk through your house while chanting your choice of hymn or prayer for 11 to 22 minutes. Play an audio recording of a prayer, chant or uplifting song in the morning or evening. When you feel stressed or sense the presence of a dark entity, pray aloud for protection.

Bells, gongs and wind chimes: Ringing bells or gongs as you walk through your living space will help break the stagnant energy. The sound raises the vibration and invites in positive energy. Hang a wind chime at the entrance of your house to ward off negative energy and create motion, harmony and peace in your dwelling.

Sound clearing with a Tibetan singing bowl.

Sound Clearing

Placing wind chimes by your front and back doors helps to dispel negative energy.

Singing bowls: Singing bowls have been used in religious ceremonies and prayer for centuries. Tibetan singing bowls are metal, but you can also use selenite singing bowls in a variety of sizes. You tap the bowl with a wooden stick. Then use the stick to trace the edge of the bowl to create a soothing vibration that relaxes the brain. Sit in the center of the room or walk through your space and play the bowl until you feel a shift to a more positive energy.

Clapping: If you're happy and you know it clap your hands! Loud, purposeful clapping can quickly disperse negative energy. Keep it simple. Walk through your space clapping about 10 to 30 times in each room to break up the stagnant, negative energy.

Protection crystals for your home

After you have cleared your space with smudging, energy sprays or sound, you can use crystals to further protect your home and energy. Selenite is a white crystal used worldwide by metaphysical practitioners for a variety of healing properties. As a protection stone, it has the ability to shield and protect from lower energies and psychic and mental attacks. Place selenite nuggets or wands over the window and door frames on the interior of your home or office to help create a protective bubble for your space.

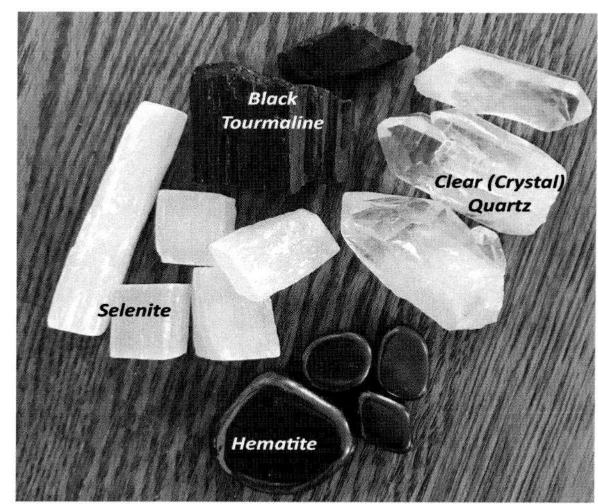

Black tourmaline is a powerful stone used for spiritual protection. It provides grounding energy to reduce stress and soothe anxiety. Place two pieces of black tourmaline at the base of your exterior doors, one on the right of the door frame and one on the left, to ward off negativity and protect from preternatural attack.

Hematite and crystal quartz, also known as clear quartz, are other powerfully protective stones to help protect your home or office. Of all the stones mentioned here, hematite and crystal quartz are the most affordable and easy to find.

Living with A Ghost

A few years after I had stepped on my spiritual enlightenment path, my family and I were moving into a new house. I had been practicing smudging and clearing the energy in spaces and houses and thought it would be important to clear the energy in this new house before we made it our home. The day before the moving truck arrived to unload our stuff, I went to the new house with all my energy clearing tools and a bold attitude thinking to myself how easy it was going to be to smudge the place.

Even though it was a hot, August day I opened every window in the house just a crack to allow the smoke to escape. Starting in the back of the house in the first floor master bathroom, I worked my way through the first floor smudging every room, wall to wall, corner to corner, top to bottom. In the kitchen, laundry room, and bathrooms I smudged inside every cabinet. I wanted to make sure this house was totally blessed and cleared of all lower energies.

As I finished the first floor I noticed a slight smell of gas. I hadn't noticed it before because if I had, I certainly wouldn't have been rolling through the house with a flaming lighter stick! It was getting much stronger, so I went back into the kitchen to check the stove. The stove was off; none of the knobs had been turned and I didn't see a flame under any of the burners. I walked outside to see if there was a gas leak from the main line, but I didn't smell it out there.

When I came back to the kitchen to check the stove again all the knobs were now turned on and the flame was lit under each burner! "Okay. That's weird!" I thought as I turned the stove off. I'm not sure why I wasn't afraid, but I just moved on upstairs. I figured that my sage would take care of whatever was turning on the stove. I was, however, too smart to light it up in the kitchen after the gas had been on!

On the second floor I continue to cover every inch of every room as thoroughly as possible. Even though the house was empty, I found random objects tucked inside drawers or wedged against a closet shelf like a picture or a conference name badge or a letter from a child's wooden alphabet puzzle. The name on the badge said Anna. The wooden puzzle letter was a capital "A." The picture was of a woman about my same age. On the back of the photo someone had handwritten the name Anna. I put all these treasures in my overalls pocket and continued about my business.

As I climbed the stairs to the third floor, unfinished attic space, I had the overwhelming sensation that someone was walking close behind me. Probably whomever was tailing me was the same energy or ghost that had turned on the stove. Ha! I'm blonde and smart! When I reached the third floor I lit my sage bundle and said "Okay. Whoever is here it's time for you to leave this is my house now." As I lifted the smoldering bundle in the air the smoke alarm when sounded! The security system voice bellowed "Fire! Fire! Leave the premises now! Fire! Fire! Leave the premises now!" It scared the hell out of me!

I had already sailed down two flights of stairs and out onto the front porch with the smoking sage bundle in my hand when I realized that I had smudged the entire house for two and half hours, passing under numerous smoke detectors, and none of them had so much as beeped!

The homeowner called my cell phone and told me that the home security company had contacted him because the alarm was going off. I told him everything was fine that I was smudging the house and I would explain later. I'm pretty sure he thought I was crazy, although he didn't ask too many questions. I sure as heck couldn't ask him if he thought there was a ghost in his house who clearly didn't want me staking claim to it. So I packed up my stuff and hoped for the best and left.

Aside from the typical moving mishaps everything went smoothly. On the third day after we moved in my son and I were sitting on the couch together watching TV in the family room. My son said "It's really hot in here Mom!" I got up to check the thermostat and it was set 72. It was another hot, August day so of course the air conditioner was on. Cool air was blowing out of the vents and everything seemed to be working fine. I turned on the ceiling fan and forgot about it.

A few minutes later he said "It's getting hotter in here! Is there something wrong with the AC?"

I checked it again and said "No, there is cold air coming out of the vents, but it is getting hot in here."

Soon it was blazing hot in the family room. The temperature on the thermostat now said 85 degrees while there was still cool air blowing out of the vents! Then I realized gas logs in the fireplace were on. The flame was really low, but the heat coming off the fireplace was incredible! I turned the logs off and blew out the pilot light. Someone or something was literally turning up the heat again to get my attention.

The following week I met our next-door neighbor. I asked her about the folks who had formerly lived in our house. She explained that the mother was about my age and had died suddenly just a year before from flu complications. She left behind a grief stricken family - her husband, a teenage son, and a seven year old daughter. I asked what her name was. She said "Anna."

I showed her the picture I found while I was smudging the house and she confirmed that in fact that was Anna. Things began to get a little more clear and a lot more interesting at this point.

Over the next few weeks Anna made herself aware to me and my family in lots of different ways. I continued to find miscellaneous trinkets around the house with her name or initials on them. One night I was in the master bedroom talking to my husband. He was laying on the bed and I was standing at the foot of the bed directly under the ceiling fan. As we talked I noticed his gaze shifted from me to the space above my head. He put his hand up to stop me from talking and then pointed toward the ceiling "Whoa! Do you see that?" The ceiling fan above me had been running at its highest speed. It had slowed down and completely come to a stop. The wall switch was still on. No human had turned off the fan!

I said "Okay Anna! We know you're here. Please turn the fan back on." I waited for a few minutes and the fan didn't come back When I left the room my husband, who was still sitting on the bed, called out to me and said "As soon as you left the room the fan slowly began spinning again and went back to normal!" Great...

Other times I would walk into my master closet and feel like I had walked through a cold spot. If I had my iPhone in my hand or in my pocket when I walked through the cold spot the phone would spontaneously make the "swoosh" sound effect like when you send an email or get a text.

I continued to smudge the house regularly. I didn't feel like Anna was any kind of threat, but I noticed that I was becoming increasingly sad and emotional. I cried a lot. I didn't want to leave the house and I could feel that my husband was also battling with some sadness too. The stove continued to turn on by itself, light bulbs blew out all the time, and something went missing almost everyday only to show up hours later in the exact space that I had remembered leaving it.

What the Cat Saw

Whenever I was alone in a room, I would sense that someone else was standing there not far away watching me. My cat Molly Francis could obviously see Anna while I can only feel her presence. When I got the feeling that Anna was in the room with me and could see but the cat sensed it too, I would ask Molly Francis, " Do you see Anna?" The cat would look at me, then look back to the space where I felt the different energy, and then look back to me as if to say "Really? You mean you can't see her?"

Every night at 9:00 P.M. Molly Francis would run up the stairs into the bedroom that had been Anna's daughters. She would sit by the window and look at bed for an hour. Then she would come out into the hall and arch and roll as if someone was petting her. She clearly got along with Anna just fine!

One night I dreamed that Anna was visiting with me in the kitchen. She said, "I want to show you something. Come with me." I followed her upstairs to the third floor, unfinished attic. When we got to the attic the space was transformed into a beautiful spa. Women there getting facials and lounging in luxurious, white robes.

When I woke up the next morning I went to the third floor attic to look around. Tucked back in the rafters, I spotted a box I hadn't noticed before. I opened it and inside was a gift box wrapped in beautiful wrapping paper and tied with an elaborate bow. The gift was addressed to Anna. I opened it and inside was a set of expensive makeup brushes and a gift certificate to a local spa. As I held the gift an overwhelming sense of sadness washed over me. I sat down on the floor and sobbed. My cat ran to my side, then she walked away, rolled onto the floor purring as if someone unseen to me was giving her the best scratches. I'm pretty sure it was her friend Anna.

Residual Negative Imprint

After living in the house for two months I noticed that my eleven year old son's personality was changing. His bedroom was the room that had been Anna's teenage son's room. My son was becoming more moody and withdrawn, very different from his usual outgoing personality. He began having bad dreams and said he saw dark things on the walls and in the corners. He didn't like being in the room alone, but he didn't want to move to another room. I did some research and realized that there was likely residual sadness, a negative imprint, attached to his room. This room was also directly across from the bedroom my cat would visit each night at 9:00 P.M.

Every time I was in his room I felt as if someone was standing just outside the door watching me. It made sense to me that Ann's son had lived there and mourned for his mother for a long time. So much sadness over an extended period of time had left a negative imprint on the room and it was affecting my son. I put a salt lamp in the room, smudged it every other day while he was gone and kept him out of the room as much as possible. The sadness was overtaking me too. Her sadness as she missed her family was unbearable. I knew she was trapped between realms and I had to figure out a way to help her cross over.

I contacted a friend who had experience with crossing earthbound spirits and made an appointment for my friend to help me cross Anna over and off this Earth plane. (The process of that is a story for another day!) Immediately after her spirit left the energy of the whole house shifted. My son was back to his normal, easy-going, happy self. The stove and the fireplace didn't turn on by themselves anymore, and the sadness I have been struggling under was finally lifted.

The entire ordeal lasted three incredible months. It taught me to trust my gut when I feel negative energy or sense that something other-worldly is in my space. I am grateful for the time with Anna and the experiences she gave me. She was the first of many earthbounds to share my homes.

Top 12 Essential Oils to Help Rid Negative Energy

1. **Frankincense** - *Oil of Truth*
2. **Lavender** - *Oil of Communication & Calm*
3. **Myrrh** - *Oil of Mother Earth*
4. **Clove** - *Oil of Boundaries*
5. **Basil** - *Oil of Renewal* (Avoid during pregnancy)
6. **Sandalwood** - *Oil of Sacred Devotion*
7. **Cypress** - *Oil of Motion & Flow*
8. **Sage** - *Oil of Ritual & Healing*
9. **Cedarwood** - *Oil of Community*
10. **Rosemary** - *Oil of Knowledge & Transition*
11. **Eucalyptus** - *Oil of Wellness*
12. **Lemon** - *Oil of Focus*

Essential Emotions, 8th Edition
ISBN 978-1-7320281-1-1, 2019

CHAPTER 8

Protect Your Light

Practical Methods for Shielding Against Darkness

We are all sponges soaking up emotional energy from other people. Sensitive people or empaths must be particularly vigilant to shield and protect themselves from intense energy. When you are around uplifting energy you will feel peace, love, happiness, and balance. If you are confronted with negativity, whether overt or covert, you may feel anxious, exhausted, confused, or physically ill. It is crucial to protect your energy and shield yourself from exposure to negativity.

Sometimes those who we trust the most can covertly steal our light. A friend who is really a *frenemy* (an enemy who poses as a friend). A spouse who is secretly jealous of you. A co-worker who is a bit too much in your business. Notice how you feel around someone. Trust your gut. If someone makes you feel uneasy, don't think twice. Protect your light.

Martin Luther King, Jr. once said "Darkness cannot drive out darkness: only light can do that." Your most powerful weapon of protection against negative energy or psychic attack is your light. What is your light? It is positive energy and love for yourself and for others. It is your faith; your belief in the Higher Power that you call on for your personal, spiritual strength. That is your light and your shield. Connect to that first to repel any darkness that attempts to steal your power. Everything has a vibrational frequency. Set your intention to raise your vibration (be positive) and focus on dialing up your light. "I only attract those who vibrate on my level or higher." Then watch as those who don't vibe as high as you are repelled!

When to protect your light

- Every day, all day; especially for empaths
- During times of emotional darkness
- When you're around toxic people
- When you sense negative energies around you such as earthbound spirits or ghosts
- When you feel physically ill or run down
- When you are under psychic attack
- When in large groups of people (concerts, conferences, gyms, airport, etc.)

Sometimes your light attracts moths, and sometimes your warmth attracts parasites.

PROTECT YOUR LIGHT.

How Entities affect your light

While other humans can drain your light, earthbound spirits (ghosts) or negative energy imprints in a room or space deplete your energy. If you've ever been alone but felt like someone or something invisible was with you, your "sixth sense" was letting you know there was an entity there. Entities are sometimes called ghosts, earthbounds, or spirits. People are usually afraid of them, but often, earthbounds - deceased humans who have not crossed over into heaven's light - are just stuck between realms and mean you no harm. Typically they get our attention just to say "hello," "goodbye." Often they are near lightworkers because they see your light and are requesting your help to depart the earth realm, which they feel trapped on. Usually they're not trying to hurt you. Instead they just want to be acknowledged.

Entities or earthbounds (ghosts) are usually found in areas of intense energy like schools, gyms, airports, hospitals, sporting events, bars, nightclubs, movie theaters, etc. They are attracted to these places to soak up the energy humans create when we are flowing with emotions. When we are amped with emotions - good or bad - earthbounds can tap into our light and get a little boost. Sometimes they come home with you from the grocery store or the gym and you don't even know it. They hang out in your space and cause your electronics to go on the fritz so that you will get angry. Sometimes they hide your keys just as you are running out for a meeting, or they scare the dog so it pees on the floor and you fly into a rage. Then they can soak up your energy and you are none the wiser.

Once you discover them they're usually easy to recognize and remove. You can usually rid yourself of an earthbound (see below Projection or a Hitchhiker) by addressing it, taking back your power or light and telling it to go. Simply say aloud and with confidence "Whatever does not have my permission to be in my space must leave now. I am wrapped in light and protection. You are not welcome here." Smudging with dry sage or incense can also help. If these tools are not enough to remove the entity contact a local healer or spiritual leader.

Sometimes entities with lower energies are energetically attracted to people who also resonate at a low frequency. These people are most vulnerable to a malevolent dark entity attachment (see below Parasite and Possessor). Simply put if your light is dim you run the risk of attracting problematic toxic entities. These toxic entities are particularly skilled at hiding and can quickly shape shift or simply disappear. They can affect your mood and the personalities of your entire household. Highly sensitive children and adults have a much stronger connection with the metaphysical world. If dark entities attach to these gifted individuals and you may not be able to remove them by yourself. In such cases it is imperative that the entities be removed. You can consult with lightworkers, ministers, or other spiritual leaders who have the ability to remove entities.

The 4 Types of Entities:

1) The Projection: This type of dark entity is an extension of another person's consciousness. It attaches to you to drain your energy or frighten you. It can happen when another human is violently angry with you, jealous, or wishes you harm. Different from an energy cord, a Projection can appear as a physical dark shadow, a dark blob shape, or smoke.

2) The Hitchhiker: This type of entity is a negative or mischievous earthbound spirit or ghost that comes near you to catch a buzz off your light. You may glimpse of them out of the corner of your eye. They might be with you for a short time or hangout with you like a double shadow indefinitely. When they are with you, you'll feel like someone is watching you.

Usually you can get rid of a Projection or a Hitchhiker by addressing it, taking back your power and telling it to go. Say aloud with confidence "Whatever does not have my permission to be in my space must leave now. I am wrapped in light and protection." Smudging can also help. If you are unable to remove the entity contact a local healer or spiritual leader.

3) The Parasite: This entity is stronger than a Hitchhiker. It leeches energy from you leaving you tired, drained, and irritable. If you've ever played with a Ouija Board or carelessly participated in a séance, you have run the risk of conjuring a Parasite. If left attached to you for too long they can create physical illness in the body which mainstream medical professionals cannot explain. Seek spiritual help from a qualified healer, minister, or spiritual leader.

4) The Possessor: The most devastating form of entity attachment is possession. There are accounts of possession in the Bible. In this case a human or animal is actually possessed or controlled by another form. Do not mess around with this energy. Seek spiritual help from a qualified healer, minister, or spiritual leader.

THOSE WHO FEAR
THE DARKNESS
HAVE NO IDEA WHAT
the LIGHT
CAN DO. -Katasai Rakshasa

How to quickly turn on your light

To protect your light you must shine brighter! Imagine you are a candle, a light bulb, the sun! Envision yourself beaming with pure, white light. Then dial up the intensity. As you turn up your light, see it fill your room. See it shine forth out of the windows. See it pushing back all the darkness until there is nothing but healing white light. Turn up your light to supernova! State your intention aloud to amplify your glow and other worldly protection: "Holy Spirit! Please wrap me in the white light. Protect me against evil and harm. Thank you!" Then go forth boldly with faith that you are protected.

Watch your words

Words have power. If you believe that thoughts and prayers can bring about healing and positive manifestations, the opposite is also true. Accidentally or intentionally, we curse others all the time. Wishing someone dead or casually saying "I wish you would go straight to hell" might be phrases we carelessly utter when we are upset, but the ramifications are powerful. When we speak angry words or harbor resentful or dark thoughts towards others our shadow "prayers" act as dark incantations.

When you focus your anger on someone else it creates a form of negative energy that transmutes into a curse or a hex. In some cultures, casting an evil eye on someone or proclaiming a hateful prayer on their behalf are actually believed to have the power to kill that person. What you put out comes back on you tenfold, so it is important to keep your words and thoughts positive. It is also imperative to understand how to protect yourself from those who wish you harm.

Psychic attacks

When you are in balance physically, mentally, emotionally and spiritually you will stand a better chance at warding off negative energy and psychic, or spiritual, attacks. Psychic attacks are energetic intrusions on the mental or physical body. An attack can develop when another person curses you, constantly thinks hateful, angry thoughts about you, or speaks ill of you to others. Psychic attacks can feel like a crushing headache, a phantom pressure or sharp pain in your back or chest, or an anxiety attack or nightmare. Extreme attacks can manifest in disabling fear or panic, extreme fatigue, or crippling emotional paralysis that will cause you to question your sanity, your spiritual beliefs, or values. They can enter your dreaming or waking mind and make some kind of detrimental impact or attempt to extract information. You may not be aware this is happening, but if you do, you need to be vigilant about keeping your protective shield up.

To release yourself from a psychic attack, first, let go of fear. Negative energies thrive on fear. Recognize the threat and then center yourself in the faith that you can overcome the dark energy that is being projected at you. The greatest defense against darkness is love and light. In this chapter you will find tools and guidance to protect yourself from negative energies and to dispel unwanted psychic attacks. Please note: some psychic attacks require trained, warrior energy and/or the assistance of a professional healer, lightworker, or shaman.

Creating protective shields

When my kids were in middle and high school they would often come home from school upset about things that had happened during the school day. Someone had bullied my son, or a mean girl had thrown Skittles at my daughter and embarrassed her on the school bus (true story). Anxiety and dread about returning to school the next day would wreck their ability to focus and

think positively. Sometimes they would get stomach aches, sore throats, or worse, they would spiral into panic attacks. Sometimes they felt nervous about their surroundings or toxic people. I understood. The corporate world was really just as awful! It was at this same time that I first began training to be a lightworker. I knew it was extremely important they learn to protect their light, so I taught them how to put up their invisible shields.

Your shield can take on any shape or form, but these examples really work for me and my children. You can quickly put up your shields with your mind's eye and fortify them throughout the day. My son's shield was a medieval knight's suit of armor. As I drove him to school, I would talk him through suiting up for the day with his imagination.

"First Honey, put on your chainmail under armor. Then strap on your sturdy breastplate, leg armor and arm shields. Next, slip on your metal shoe coverings and gloves. Don't forget your helmet! Now turn up your protection light inside your armor and know that it is going to be a great day!"

If you're in a highly charged situation or out in public, visualize a translucent pink bubble around you - just like Glenda the Good Witch in The Wizard of Oz! If outside threats or energies strike at you, they can't penetrate your protection bubble. Nothing can get inside to harm you! Better still, you're totally shielded from absorbing others' energies. Anytime you feel threatened or uneasy, simply close your eyes and envision yourself in your protection bubble.

My daughter's shield took the form of a disco, hamster ball! She imagined herself safely inside the giant disco ball. She could confidently roll through the halls of her high school inside her imaginary ball. Any negative energy thrown her way was deflected back on the sender by the mirrors on the ball. Get creative with your protection shields!

My favorite shield is one I call The Invisible Cactus. As an empath and an ambivert (sometimes introvert, sometimes extrovert) there were occasions when I wanted to slip into places and not interact with others. If I wanted to get in and out of the school open house and not take on any of the energy of the folks there. Bam! I tossed up my Invisible Cactus shield! I imagined myself as real cactus. If anyone got too close to my energy field, they would get pricked on my spines and back off. Try it for yourself! I swear it works.

Once, I walked into a meeting hall filled with over eager conference goers. I really didn't want to hob-nob with anyone that day. So I began repeating to myself in silence

THE ARMOR OF GOD

Ephesians 6:10-19

10 Finally, be strong in the Lord and in the strength of His might.

11 Put on the full armor of God, so that you will be able to stand firm against the schemes of the devil.

12 For our struggle is not against the flesh and blood, but against the rulers, against the powers, against the world forces of wickedness in the heavenly places.

13 Therefore, take up the full armor of God, so that you will be able to resist in the evil day, and having done everything to stand firm.

14 Stand firm therefore, having girded your loins with truth and having put on the breastplate of righteousness,

15 and having shod your feet with the preparation of the gospel of peace;

16 in addition to all, taking up the shield of faith with which you will be able to extinguish all the flaming arrows of the evil one.

17 And take the helmet of salvation, and the sword of the Spirit, which is the word of God.

18 With all prayer and petition pray at all times in the Spirit, and with this in view, be on the alert with all perseverance and petition for all the saints,

19 and pray...

IN THE BIBLE, EPHESIANS 6:10-19 TELLS US HOW TO PREPARE OURSELVES TO DO BATTLE AGAINST THE INVISIBLE WAR WITH DARKNESS THAT SWIRLS AROUND US BY PUTTING ON THE FULL ARMOR OF GOD.

"I am the Invisible Cactus. I am the Invisible Cactus," and watched as the sea of people parted as I approached! Even my co-workers looked right through me as if I was not even there!

Disarm with a glance

"The Evil Eye" is a legendary curse some believe can be cast on to another person by simply giving them a mean or malevolent glare. A stern glare from someone could be considered hexing them or giving "the Evil Eye." It is usually cast on to someone when they are unaware. Many cultures across Europe, Asia and parts of South America and the Caribbean believe that receiving the evil eye will cause you bad luck, severe illness, or even death. Others believe the evil eye is a kind of talisman that actually mirrors back ill will to those who wish to do harm to you.

When to Shield Your Light to Increase your Peace

Every day, all day
If you're an empath or intuitive
During times of emotional darkness
When you remember trauma
When you dread seeing certain people
When you're around toxic people
When you sense negative energies around you such as earthbounds or ghosts
When you feel physically ill or run down
When you are under psychic attack
When you're in large groups of people (concerts, conferences, airports, etc.)

Some ancient cultures believe you can also protect yourself with just a glance. When you want to protect yourself or disarm someone, give them what pop culture now refers to as "the Up/Down."

You've seen it, or you've probably done it to someone! You look them square in the eyes, then roll your gaze down the length of their body to their feet, back up to their head, and then back down to their feet. It's that "Mean Girl" move that feels like someone just called you ugly and slapped you by just rolling their eyes! It's also a simple, ancient tool for disarming someone before they psychically attack you. A good offense is the best defense and the eyes have it.

"You don't show emotion, say anything interesting, or disclose any personal information. Nor do you ask questions or participate in conversations, except for brief factual replies. Limit your answers to a few syllables or a nod."

-Darlene Lancer, JD, MFT, *Psychology Today*

THE GRAY ROCK METHOD

A POWERFUL PROTECTIVE SHIELD AGAINST NARCISSISTS

CHAPTER 9

Shielding Against Narcissists

The Gray Rock Method

A narcissists is a particularly difficult type of person who can feed on your light. It's not a coincidence that empaths are often attracted to narcissists without realizing it. Who has the most light? Empaths! Until you've dealt with a narcissist, you just don't know how powerful your shields need to be. Over the years, I have found The Gray Rock Method, a psychological technique of shielding, is particularly effective in dealing with a manipulative person, a narcissist, sociopath, or individuals with borderline personality disorders. The Gray Rock Method is similar to the strategies I gave my kids to create protective shields. You simply imagine you are a gray rock. What is interesting about a gray rock, you ask? Nothing. Nothing at all. With this shielding method you act like a gray rock and become as bland, uninteresting and unresponsive as possible so you stop attracting the narcissist's attention, stop feeding their drama until they lose interest in you.

Darlene Lancer, JD, MFT states, "You don't show emotion, say anything interesting, or disclose any personal information. Nor do you ask questions or participate in conversations, except for brief factual replies. Limit your answers to a few syllables or a nod. Say "maybe" or "I don't know." Additionally, make yourself plain and unattractive, so your partner gains no pleasure in showing you off or being seen with you. This maneuver removes the narcissist's "narcissistic supply."

"Using The Gray Rock Method, you make yourself seem so boring that the other person has no interest in you and will look elsewhere to get their needs met. Even if you're accused, you might agree or say nothing. Your nonresistance makes it harder for them to project onto you. The idea is to blend into the background, like a gray rock." Try it. It takes practice to not be triggered by the continued psychological assault from a toxic person, but I swear it works.

When the narcissist is angry with you or feels they have lost control over you, they may connect to you through toxic energy cords and you could suffer from a psychic or psychological attack. It can come on fast and may feel like a migraine, nausea, depression, or a panic attack. Scan your energy and trust the first person who comes to mind when you ask "Who is attacking me?" It is crucial to understand this: the only reason you are being psychically attacked is because you are allowing someone into your energy to steal your power. Focus on what you are doing, consciously or subconsciously, to create or attract the psychic attack. Consider how you have given away your light. Review the chapter on cutting energetic cords, remove the cords and focus on healing the part of you that creates the ability for someone to attack you. William Lee Rand, Reiki Master states, "Often, as we come into our own power, we may not be confident because perhaps we have misused power in the past. This may cause us to be attacked by ourselves or by others who feel threatened by our increased power."

Narcissists and codependency

Codependency is a behavioral condition where one person in a relationship has excessive emotional or psychological reliance on their partner. One of the primary traits of codependency is an extreme and unhealthy reliance on other people for approval and a sense of identity. Often you don't even realize you are codependent.

Codependency and narcissistic abuse go hand in hand. Do you feed off others' neediness, or devote all your energy to your partner? You could be codependent. If you are, it can be more difficult for you to take back your light. Signs of codependency include:

- Allow others to make decisions for you
- Difficulty putting your needs first
- You have trouble speaking your mind
- You value others' approval more than you value yourself
- Poor self-esteem
- You fear abandonment
- Constant need for approval
- Unhealthy dependence on relationships, even at your own cost
- Exaggerated sense of responsibility for the other's actions and outcomes

If you think you are in involved with a narcissist - a partner, a parent, a boss - seek guidance from a therapist. If you believe your spouse or partner is a narcissist go to therapy alone first. Do not attempt couples therapy before you have the tools to handle the narcissist. A therapist can help you see patterns in your relationships, determine if you are prone to codependency, and help you take steps to form a healthy sense of self complete with healthy boundaries.

CHAPTER 10

Energy Cords

Take Back your Power

Have you ever been thinking about someone when out of the blue they contact you? They say, "Hey! You have been on my mind!" It may feel serendipitous, but this is an example of a positive energy cord connection. Picture a baby connected by the umbilical cord to its mother's womb. Invisible energy cords connect us to other humans in the same way and allow for the exchange of emotional energy between our etheric bodies. Sometimes referred to as cords of attachment, energy cords are particularly strong between people who are closest to us: family members, partners, spouses, friends, and colleagues. Both love and hate create equally strong cords.

What are energy cords?

There are two types of energy cords: positive cords and negative, toxic cords. A positive cord is healthy, like the connection between a loving parent and child. It allows for the flow of unconditional love, emotional support, balanced relationships, and mutual respect. We connect positively to others through prayer, words and thoughts of affirmation and praise, fond memories, and general well-meaning feelings of abundance and love. These cords, fortified by love and good intentions, help us to thrive.

A negative or toxic cord binds us to another person in dark energy. Are you often angry at others and allow their actions or inactions to irritate you even when they are not around? Are you having a difficult time getting over a breakup even if you know the relationship was toxic? Do memories, both good and bad, of ex lovers or spouses frustratingly haunt your mind? When you're in the presence of a friend, co-worker or family member does it make you feel drained? These are signs that you have negative energy cords that need to be removed.

Left attached, these cords can create feelings of fear, self-loathing, anxiety, rage, insecurity, even paranoia, and can allow for psychic manipulation. Physical symptoms may include severe headache, migraine, nausea or flu-like symptoms, dehydration, acute pain at the point of cord attachment. It is important to remove your toxic cords frequently and even daily during times of stress and despair. Failure to remove negative cords can be detrimental to your mental and physical health. You may be unable to completely cut a toxic person out of your life, but you can increase your shields against them and remove the negative cords.

Common energy cord connections:

- Parents, siblings, other family members
- Sexual partners, spouses, ex lovers, past life connections
- Negative, vengeful, jealous friends, co-workers, classmates, neighbors
- Bullies, energy vampires, verbal abuse
- Sexual abuse, domestic violence

The love connection

Energy cords between lovers and ex lovers are very powerful and are amplified by sexual intercourse. When you have sex with someone you have an energy exchange that aligns your chakras with your partner's. When you connect with a lover physically and emotionally energetic cords are formed to bond you to your partner. In a balanced relationship, this connection can be wonderful and help to increase your loving bond; but in a toxic or broken relationship a negative exchange of energy continues along these channels. That can be extremely detrimental to one or both partner's emotional well-being. It may inhibit you from releasing the ex lover from your energy field and pre-

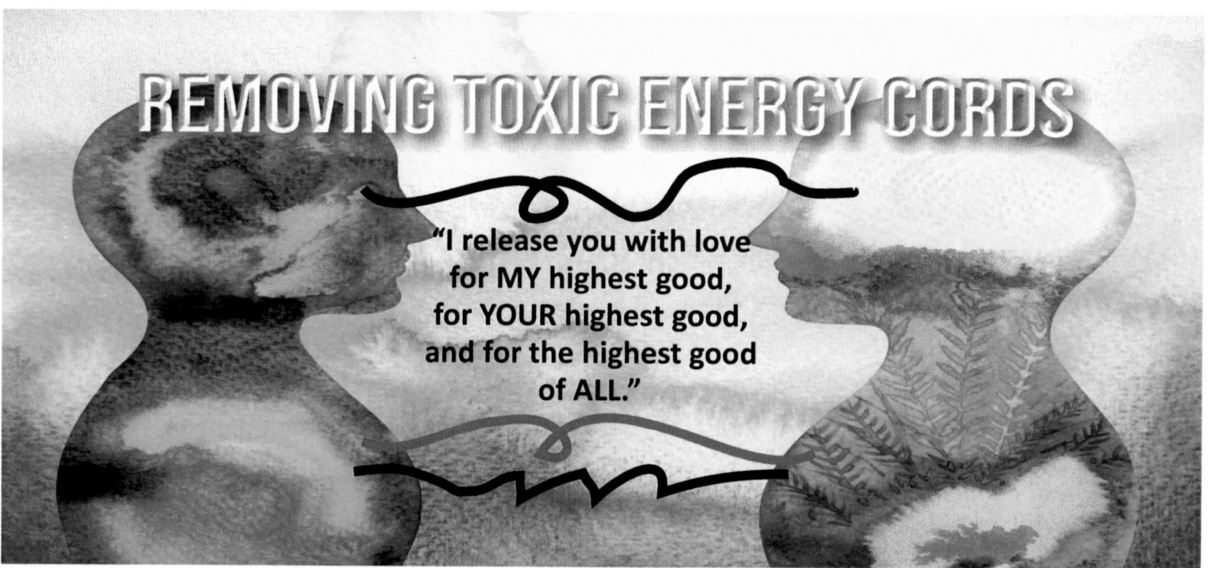

How to Remove Energy Cords in 10 Easy Steps

1. Determine the location of the cord. Where do you feel pain in your physical or emotional body?
2. Identify the source of the cord you want to remove. Who is your cord attached to? Trust the first person who comes to mind. Think about your close relationships, people with whom you've been in recent arguments. Who keeps coming to mind? Is there an incident you need to release?
3. Call on Archangel Michael for protection and assistance with cord cutting and removal. State your request either aloud or in thought "Archangel Michael, I call upon you and the ministry of angels now. Please cut the cords of negativity and fear that are draining my energy and vitality."
4. If you know the person's name who has a cord connected to you, state their name in the request.
5. Imagine Archangel Michael using his sword to cut the cords attached to you.
6. Sit quietly and breathe deeply while he cuts your cords. Trust the process.
7. Ask Archangel Michael to (painlessly) dig out the residual cord stump with the tip of his sword, and to cauterize the wound site with healing gold light. He will send healing energy through the severed cords to both you and the other person.
8. Imagine yourself bathed in white light, protected and free from any unhealthy connections.
9. Remember to give gratitude to Archangel Michael for his help!
10. Repeat daily or several times a day during times of relationship conflict or stress.

Sometimes you will need additional help to remove energetic cords of attachment from narcissists or abusive people. If you feel you are unable to remove the energy cords permanently or need help with a thorough emotional release, seek assistance from a healer, lightworker or shaman.

vent you from moving forward in life. It can also cause you to bring negative emotions and detrimental behaviors into your future relationships.

How to remove toxic energy cords

When you neglect to remove toxic cords, the result is like having a slow leak in your tire. Depending on the power and the determination of the person on the other end of the cord, you will continuously be drained and depleted until you remove it. With practice you can learn to remove toxic energy cords from intense relationships. Sometimes you will need additional help to remove energy cords embedded in you from a narcissist or abusive person. If you are unable to remove the energy cords permanently on your own or need help with a thorough emotional release, seek assistance from a healer, lightworker or shaman.

If you feel the person you are attached to is a karmic partner, twin-flame or past-life connection, or you just simply cannot get them out of your life use the Unhooking Method. The Unhooking Method is a profoundly powerful and healing exercise to help you reclaim your light. When you have a deep emotional attachment to someone, the energetic cords connecting you both are rooted deep in your emotional body. An example of a positive attachment would be between a mother and child who have a healthy, loving relationship. A toxic connection may form between lovers when one wants to end the relationship and the other does not.

Such cords can be very difficult to remove whether the relationship is romantic or not. When the relationship is codepen-

dent, abusive, obsessive, or oppressive, you will need to exercise a deeper cord removal to free both you and the person connected to you. The Unhooking Meditation helps you release the hold you have on each other and take back your light.

A few years ago, I went through an especially traumatic break-up. It was sudden and scary and violent. In an instant, my life was turned upside down. I had practiced successful cord-cutting for years, but this time it wasn't working. My soul connection to this love was too deep. My spiritual counselor shared with me the unhooking process. She suggested I try it to relieve some of the post traumatic stress symptoms I was experiencing months after the break-up.

The first time I attempted the unhooking it was incredibly spiritual and profound. I went into a deep meditation. As I called forth the image of my ex love to announce that I was about to unhook our cords, I began sobbing, and was consumed in hurt and loss. My meditation spiraled into memories of our love and happiness. In my imagination I took back the hooks I had placed in him, and gave him back the hooks he had placed in me. My first unhooking meditation lasted almost an hour. Afterwards I was exhausted, but felt lighter and more composed.

Over the following months, whenever I felt particularly sad over the break-up, I would repeat the process several times. Each time my higher soul connected to his, new memories appeared to be cleared and released. Each time was a little bit easier until eventually there was nothing left to connect me but good memories and the understanding of the lessons we gave each other.

The Unhooking Method and Meditation

Center yourself in a calm, meditative state. Visualize thick, mucus colored, slimy cords attached to your body. On the ends of the cords are metal hooks that pierce your skin, latch through your rib cage and fasten deep within your body. Are the cords attached at a site that causes you physical or emotional pain? Take a deep breath. Let's remove them.

WARNING:

Using the Unhooking Method can be an emotionally powerful experience. After a painful break-up or trauma you may have to repeat this process several times for thorough cleansing and release.

Determine the source of the cords. Imagine that person sitting in front of you. Call their name and draw their soul before you. Your higher self is going to have a conversation with their higher self, soul to soul.

Now look at their body. See the cords and hooks that are attached to them coming from you. What color are the cords you have in them? Where are the hooks on their body?

Take another deep breath. Announce to your person: "[Insert person's name] I have called you here today to remove the hooks that you have placed in me, the hooks that I have allowed you to connect to my soul, and the hooks I have placed in you."

Next, visualize yourself detaching the hooks and cords from your own body. With each hook you remove, state what incident or emotion you are unhooking from and return it to the other person. Hooks will be both good and bad memories. For example, as you remove each hook you might say:

"I am giving you back this hook and with it all the pain you've caused me."

"I return this hook to you and with it the times I allowed you to make me feel devalued."

"I release myself from the love you once gave me that no longer exists."

"I give you back the times you were kind to my family and friends."

"I give you made me feel loved."

"I give you back the fun times we spent together doing ____."

As you unhook, you will give back both negative and positive memories and experiences. The good and the bad as you free yourself from all connection with this person. Dredging up these memories will be emotional. Don't give up. Say everything you need to say to them, face to face, as your soul speaks to theirs.

Next it's time to retrieve the hooks you have placed in the other person. Go through the same process imagining yourself grasping hook after hook from their body and proclaiming what you are taking back with it.

"I take back all the love and trust I gave you."

"I take back my power and break the chains of codependency."

"I take back the ways I tried to make you happy and fulfilled."

"I take back the ugly things I have wished on you."

"I take back the days I trusted you to protect my heart and soul."

"I take back the ways I tried to make you happy.

Allow yourself to flow with this spiritual conversation. Take as long as you need to say what you need to say. When you are finished removing all the hooks you can presently see, release yourself from your karmic connections to the other person. State aloud or in your thoughts,

"I am releasing all connection to you in the past, in the present, and in the future. Our karmic ties are now dissolved. I hereby break all karmic loyalty contracts. Our karmic debts are now paid. I release you with love for my highest good, for your highest good, and for the highest good of all.
So be it."

Be gentle with yourself after this meditation. Put up your energy shields. Do whatever you can to raise your vibration. Soak in a warm, Epsom Salt bath with essential oils. Be aware that often ***when you do this powerful unhooking and retrieval ritual, the other person will feel it on a soul level***. They may approach you in your dreams or contact you shortly afterwards to attempt to reestablish the connection and re-hook the cords. If possible, resist contact with them. Put your shields up and repeat the above process again. If the person you are unhooking from is narcissistic, you can use the Gray Rock Method described on page 45 to help shield you from further connection or abuse.

CHAPTER 11

Crystals for Protection

Rock Solid Ways to Ground and Shield

Crystals are powerful, natural healing tools that can provide spiritual protection against other humans or malevolent spirits. The right crystals can also protect your aura and prevent psychic attack. Using crystal protection helps you to shake off these lower energies more easily. Crystals work to deflect or absorb dark energy and align with your root chakra to help ground and protect you. If you're not familiar with crystals, a good rule of thumb in selecting protection crystals is to choose the black or dark ones.

Crystal bracelets are a fun and fashionable way to experience their healing properties everyday.

Everyday protection

Crystals work best when worn against the skin. Bracelets and necklaces are good choices, or you can tuck a smooth, tumbled crystal in your bra. Place a stone in your pants or shirt pocket, or carry a thumb stone (meditation stone) with you. Each crystal has a unique frequency and healing property. You can wear or carry as many different stones as you wish as they work well in combination.

Protect Your home

To protect your home from negativity, create a boundary by setting up a crystal grid. Place one piece of black tourmaline at each of the external corners of your property or against the exterior corners of the house. You can also put two pieces of black tourmaline or hematite at the outside base of all exterior doors to further block negativity.

To protect a room, after smudging the space, put a piece of black tourmaline or hematite in each of the corners of the room and at the corners of exterior doors. Place a piece of selenite over each interior door and window frame.

Ward off clingy people & energy vampires

Is someone being excessively clingy or negatively attached to you? You can use black obsidian to cut negative energy cords from others and create a border of protection around your aura. Use a black obsidian arrowhead, or a piece that has a point, and trace a protective outline around your entire body. Set your intention to cut the energy cords from the specific person. You can also allow your intuition to guide you to determine where the cord is attached to your aura; then gently place the crystal on your skin at that area, and with a cutting motion, sever the connection.

Relief from nightmares and insomnia

Are you suffering from nightmares or insomnia? Psychic attacks and caustic energy from other people and negative event imprints on your home and property can seriously affect your sleep. Dark energy collects in chaotic spaces, so first clear the clutter in your room and home. Next, smudge the entire house with emphasis on your bedroom. Place a piece of black tourmaline in each corner of the room. Then place a piece of selenite over the interior door frame, atop each window frame, or on the window sill.

Creating a crystal grid around your bed can help. Place a piece of black tourmaline on the floor by each bed post. Then, create an outline of the bed on the floor just under the edge of the bed, using alternating dark and light crystals. Fluorite, rose quartz, angelite, amethyst, or smoky quartz are good choices for the light crystals to provide healing, uplifting support. Any of the dark stones listed in this chapter are effective for protection. Set your intention that your home and bedroom are safely shielded from all lower energies.

Be sure to recharge the crystals in your room each month and reset them. You can clear them by smudging, running them under water, setting them in the sunlight or by other methods found on page 76.

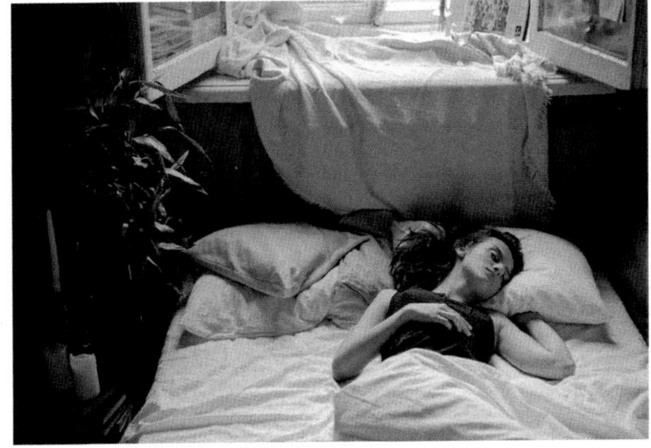

Dark Entity in Suburbia

The sound of a car door slamming on the street in front of the house woke me up at 3:30 A.M. I was sleeping over at my fiancé's house. He lived in a new, suburban neighborhood in Raleigh, North Carolina where the houses were close together and close to the street. Car doors slamming and traffic noises in the night were common. As I woke from a deep sleep it took a few minutes for my eyes to adjust to the night. A street lamp shone through the window and illuminated the bedroom. I preferred to sleep in a dark room, so the brightness really annoyed me. Suddenly an odd feeling washed over me and I felt like someone was in the room with us. I rolled over onto my back slowly so as not to wake up Rick.

Then I saw it. In the upper right corner of the bedroom was a large, dark mass. It was formless. Just a blob of black matter floating, undulating in the corner against the ceiling of the far bedroom wall opposite our bed. I can't explain how I knew that it was watching us, but it was. I didn't want to move or wake Rick with a fright. The big, black blob started to move out away from the wall towards our bed. It grew a bit larger and then started moving along the white wall and ceiling toward the bedroom door on the left. As it moved it became more three dimensional and extended off the wall now. It began expanding into the room, growing larger and it was coming towards us. I was scared to death! It was becoming darker and more solid; oozing and shifting like thick gooey, black tar.

As it hovered in the air about 5 feet from the foot of the bed I sat up and said in a whispered hiss, "Stay back! Stay away from us! I am wrapped in the white light of Christ!" The dark entity stopped approaching just as Rick woke up startled and confused.

He said, "What is the matter?! What's wrong?"

I pointed to the black thing and said, "Pray with me! Now! Don't be afraid. Help me command it to leave."

I sat up taller and said firmly, "Get out of this room! Leave this house! I am wrapped in the holy light of Christ. I call on Archangel Michael to protect us from whatever darkness you are. You do not belong here! Leave now!"

With that the dark entity slowly recoiled. It rolled along the ceiling back to the far bedroom wall. Then it slid down the wall and out the bedroom door.

I wish I could say I was brave enough to follow it as it floated out of the bedroom, but I was still in shock. About 15 minutes later I convinced Rick to go downstairs to just look around. We got up our courage to leave the bedroom, turning on all the lights as we searched the house. Thankfully, we didn't see anything strange and eventually settled down enough to go back to sleep.

The dark entity never came back that night or any other time at Rick's house. Afterwards I saw similar dark entities in my home on three occasions - once in the daytime and twice at night. Another time during the night in a posh hotel room in Charleston, South Carolina, and once more at night at a friend's beach house on the North Carolina coast. Each time I called out for protection from God and Archangel Michael and was filled with the courage to dispel the darkness before me.

As I think back on what was going on in my life each time I saw a dark entity, I can see a pattern in the occurrences. In five out of those six instances I was going through some serious personal struggles in my waking life. I was consumed by sadness and fear over life events that were out of my control. I can now see clearly that in these times, my light had gone out, allowing the darkness to try to come in. I have learned the importance of keeping my light shining bright. Each day I establish both physical and spiritual boundaries to protect myself and my light.

When I was a child, my parents or grandparents would tuck me into bed at night. They taught me to say my prayers before falling asleep. "Now I lay me down to sleep. I pray to the Lord my soul to keep." That habit has stuck with me through my lifetime. I still say my prayers every night when I go to bed and I always make sure to ask my guardian angels to watch over me and my loved ones and hold us in light to protect us from darkness.

Crystal Quartz The Rock Star in the Crystal Universe
Crystal Quartz, or Clear Quartz, is THE most powerful healing stone and energy amplifier on earth. It's been used to power watches and electronics for decades! Its superpower is in its ability to raise your energy to the highest level possible. Quartz is almost the most versatile healing crystal there is and can be used for any cleansing, energizing or healing.
Protection: Clear quartz protects against negative energy and will transmute it to positive energy.
Home: Clear quartz will help your family to live together in harmony. It helps instill a sense of optimism and purpose when times are difficult.
Psychic: Clear quartz will amplify any healing or psychic power. It is also suitable for communicating with angels and spirit guides, and can be used for aura work.
Environment: Clear quartz will send environmental healing energy to anywhere it is needed on the planet.
Animals: Use clear quartz with old animals to help give them an energy and health boost.
Children: All children should be given a piece of clear quartz to be kept throughout life. It will gradually increase in power and act as their own personal talisman.
psychic-revelation.com

Best Crystals for Protection

Black Tourmaline is the most powerful crystal for protection and repelling lower frequencies. It cleanses and purifies energy, balances the chakras, and forms a protective shield around the body or space. Black Tourmaline is particularly powerful against psychic attacks. It transmutes the energy to increase vitality and restore positive emotional outlook.

Black Obsidian is extremely effective at blocking negative psychic and spiritual influences. Placed under the bed or a pillow, it can draw out mental stress and tension and provide a calming effect. However, be prepared, it will also bring up the root causes for the stress in order for it to be resolved. Meditate with black obsidian to help uncover lies, remove emotional blocks, and release destructive habits. It is important to clean the stone under running water each time you use it as it will soak up so much negative energy.

Hematite has a metallic sheen and high iron content, and not only absorbs lower frequency energy, but it also creates a protective shield around you that reflects negative energies back to the sender. It is one of the best stones for grounding both the body and soul and is often used during out-of-body journeying. Hematite removes self-limiting beliefs, boosts confidence, helps to overcome addictions and bad habits. It ground the user helps deflect others' negative comments or judgments.

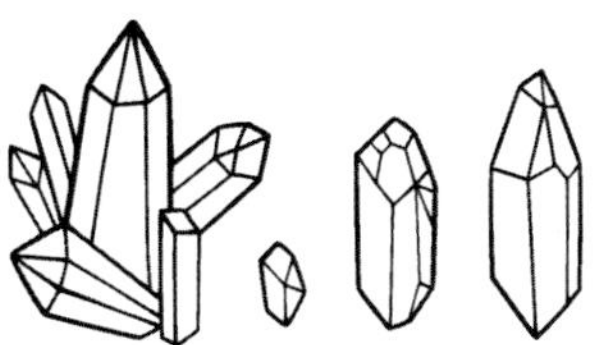

Tiger's Eye is both stabilizing and protective. It can be carried as a talisman against curses and ill wishes. It enhances psychic abilities, is powerful for releasing fears, and enhances clarity of intention. Tiger's Eye can also help you move forward with life, achieve goals, manifest money, or maintain a positive attitude. Wear on the right side of the body for short periods.

Fluorite is highly protective on a psychic level. Fluorite can cloak your aura, which hides you from psychic attack! It dissolves chaotic mind chatter. It aids in discernment and guards against manipulation and toxic mental influence. It is extremely powerful against computer and electromagnetic stress. Fluorite transmutes the energy, grounds it, stabilizes the user. Fluorite works hard so it needs to be cleaned often.

Smoky Quartz is the most powerful healing stone and energy amplifier on earth. It's superpower is its ability to raise your energy to the highest level possible. If you are a lightworker, a clairvoyant, or perform spiritual ceremonies, Smoky Quartz provides grounding, amplification and protection from dark entities. It provides clear insight and alleviates dark thoughts, fear, depression, nightmares, and desires to self harm. It is very effective when placed under your pillow or near electronics to block harmful electromagnetic waves.

Amethyst is one of the most spiritual of stones. It connects the user's third eye and crown chakra to high vibration which will protect your energy field against psychic attack and negativity. It guards against psychic attack by transmuting the bad energy into love. It increases psychic gifts, calms the mind and enhances mental clarity. It is used to break from addictive relationships, encouraging peace of mind and inner strength.

Each month put your crystals and crystal jewelry out in the full moon light to recharge.

CHAPTER 12

Angels

Heavenly Protection from The A-Team

I work with angel energy every day in combination with other healing arts tools and have witnessed incredible results. I believe in angels and I have felt their healing and protective presence. Several world religions recognize angels as creations and messengers of God. Angels play a big role in the religious texts and doctrines Judaism, Islam, the Baha'i Faith, Catholic and Orthodox churches, and protestant Christianity just to name a few. In fact, Pope John Paul II made a series of talks "on the subject of angels, in which emphasized that 'they do exist' and 'have a fundamental role to play in the unfolding of human events'" as noted in David Connolly's book "In Search of Angels." Connolly also states "The Vatican newspaper printed an entire sermon by Cardinal Angelo Sodano, Vatican secretary of state, under the headline "Guardian Angels Guide Us and Cheer Us on the Path of Life."

Angels are typically considered to be kind, supernatural beings, who act as intercessors between God and humans. Their roles include guiding and protecting humans and fulfilling tasks assigned by God. They are non-denominational and help anyone regardless of their religious or non-religious beliefs. Angels work behind the scenes in our lives to protect us from physical harm, guard us from evil, or provide guidance or inspiration if doing so would help accomplish God's purposes for your life. They stand ready to assist you at any moment and all you have to do is ask. When you find yourself in physical or spiritual danger, call on the angels.

You can simply speak aloud or think, "Angels help me!" Calling on angels to help you is not praying to them. Angels are the creation of God. You pray to God, but you call on your angels for assistance.

The Archangels

It is the Archangels' job to oversee the guardian angels. Archangels can be in an infinite number of places simultaneously and can help an infinite number of humans without limit to space, time or location. Most of their names end in "el", which in Hebrew translates to "of God." The archangels listed here are a few of the main angels often associated with protection and overcoming strife.

Archangel Michael's name translates to "One who is like God." He is considered to be the head of the angels and one of the most powerful. He carries his sword of truth and defends all things that are pure. He is a warrior against demons and darkness. Call Michael's name aloud when you are in a threatening situation and he will protect you. You can ask him to wrap his blue cloak around you to protect you from danger of any type or to assist you with major life changes.

Archangel Gabriel's name means "God is my strength." Sometimes Gabriel is portrayed as a male, others times as female. She is the messenger angel who delivers divine messages. Gabriel supports you in times of change. She helps to overcome procrastination and supports writers, teachers, journalists, speakers, and all earthly messengers. Call on her for support with communication, pregnancy, child conception, and speaking your truth.

Archangel Chamuel's name means "One who seeks God." He is the Archangel of peace and can assist in all areas of emotional distress and decision making. Call on Archangel Chamuel to help you raise your vibrational energy, to ease your anxiety, to release stress about situations that are out of your control and to surround you with love. He assists with relationships, new jobs, or any lost item.

Archangel Ariel's name means "Lion or Lioness of God." Ariel is the angel of Earth, the natural world, and the animal kingdom. Call on Ariel to help you feel calm and grounded and to soothe any fears. Ariel helps to open us up to greater abundance in our lives. She offers protection from disease, severe pain, and psychic attack.

Archangel Uriel's name means "God is my light." Uriel helps illuminate your thought process. He helps with troubleshooting and problem solving. If you need protection from the bitterness and jealousy of others, Uriel can help you avoid these negative people. Call on Uriel to help you with motivation, inspiration, and clarity. Uriel is also the angel of students. Call on him to help you recall material when taking a test!

Archangel Metatron's name means "angel of the Presence." Metatron is one of only two archangels who were once human men. He is believed to have been the prophet Enoch. He is the angel of children and works to protect them and assist in their spiritual understanding. Call on him to help you guide and protect your children on earth and in heaven.

How to call on your angels

Connecting with the angels is easy; you simply ask them for help. You don't have to say it out loud, you can just think it. There is no protocol or ritual – no need for candles, incense, oils, or complicated scripts. All you need to do is to ask them for assistance and they will go to work on your behalf. Angels follow the Universal Law of Request and won't interfere with you until you ask them. They will always respect your free will and allow you to make choices and learn life lessons. Angels are essentially light and vibrate on a much higher frequency than humans. You have to provide them a portal of light with which to reach you. All the methods discussed in the book about how to turn up your light come into play here. If you're consumed by negative energies– anger, fear, despair – light can't penetrate it. The angels can't easily communicate with you when your vibe is low.

Open up to the light by having concrete trust and faith that there is always heavenly, angelic help available for us. Call out and ask. "Angels! I need you! Please help me to see a way out of this situation. Please

Angelic Warning

The first time I remember hearing angel guidance I was cooking dinner. In hindsight I realize that I had been hearing them my entire life, I just thought it was my own subconscious inner dialogue.

I'm sure you know what I mean. Perhaps you've been lying in bed at night, just before you fall asleep you hear "Go lock the front door." You're almost certain you already locked the door. You do it every night, right? Then you hear it again. "Go lock the front door." You ignore the thought and convince yourself that of course the door is locked, only to wake up the next morning and discover not only was the door unlocked, but it was left half open because your child's tennis shoe got dropped on the threshold. Now the cat has escaped and the house is full of mosquitoes, not to mention the house was unsecured all night long!

On this particular evening when I clearly heard my guardian angels I was standing at my stove, cooking dinner for my 6 year old son when I heard a small voice inside my mind say "Close the garage door." I thought "The garage door is closed," and I stirred the pot of couscous. Then I heard it again. "Close the garage door." "It's closed." I thought again. It's always closed. I drive into the garage. Park the car. Put down the door and then get out of the car. Today was no different. "The door is closed," I rationalized.

As I spread out the frozen chicken tenders on the baking sheet I heard it even louder this time "Close the garage door."

I stubbornly ignored it again. I could have easily taken four steps across the kitchen to make sure the garage door was down, but I didn't. As I served our plates for dinner I heard it again even louder still. "CLOSE the garage door!" As I put the plates on our TV trays "CLOSE THE GARAGE door!" As I sat down on the couch with my son to watch Nickelodeon and eat the voice was emphatic. "CLOSE THE GARAGE DOOR! CLOSE! THE! GARAGE! DOOR! CLOSE THE GARAGE DOOR!"

Suddenly there was an intruder in my house! He burst in from the garage, stormed across the kitchen to the den where we sat stunned and surprised. My life would have taken a different turn if I had listened that night. The intruder broke into my home and almost strangled me to death. Police, arrest, emergency room, restraining orders, attorneys, court dates, a criminal trial, lots of therapy, and so much trauma. My life would have been different if I had listened to the angel warnings. We humans certainly have to learn the hard way.

protect me from darkness and surround me in light and God's love." Ask for what you need and trust help will arrive. Look for signs for your angels to communicate to you, and always thank them for the help.

How to hear your angels

Your experience with angels might include new ideas, revelations, or a change in feeling or emotions. Angel messages will never be frightening or cause you to harm yourself or others. They are always encouraging and empowering and will be assertive and not alarming even when warning you of danger. There can be a sense that someone is talking to you and you will know that it is not your own subconscious mind. They will encourage you to take positive human steps toward an action, or it may be a simple directive like "Go speak to him."

Often angels will speak to you through music. Have you ever been listening to the radio and heard a series of songs in which the lyrics seemed to speak directly to you? That's not a coincidence. It's your angels trying to communicate to you to help you raise your vibration and turn up your light.

Have you ever overheard a conversation between strangers and it seemed to be meant specifically for your ears? It was! Angels will get messages to you through others' conversations, billboards, book titles, and song lyrics. My favorite way angels speak to me is out of the mouths of children. Children can often be inspired to share the most profound messages with us as guided by the angels.

Many lightworkers, like myself, experience a high pitched ringing in one ear when angels are trying to talk to us. Trust me, when it first began happening to me regularly I visited my doctor to rule out tinnitus (a disturbance of the auditory nerve)! Sometimes the tone is so shrill it feels like sharp pain or a pinch on my eardrum. This happens when they really want to get my attention. The ringing alerts me to listen to the conversations going on around me right at that moment, to pay attention to the news or messages I am experiencing right then, to notice my surroundings, or it is a download of info that will come in handy in the near future. When I am really on my path or "in the groove" like when I was writing this book, the ringing is pretty constant. If it gets too loud, I say "Thank you for all the info. Help me discern the intuitive messages and when I need to act on them; but could you turn down the volume, please." Within a few seconds the ringing subsides!

Angel Assistance at the Courthouse

The first time I remember calling my angels for assistance I was at the courthouse. It had been a hideous 18 months. I was mentally and emotionally exhausted from a long, divorce proceeding with a side order of criminal assault trial. It's nearly impossible to finalize a divorce when you have a restraining order against your ex, much less effectively co-parent with them. Now the divorce was done and the criminal trial was over. Just when I thought I could get on with my life - oh, no such luck! My ex-husband decided to take me back to court and continue the argument. I had spent so much money in attorney fees and wasted too much time in court. I was completely fried.

I was trying to save money instead of spending more of it on legal fees, so I chose to try to file the Response to Motion paperwork myself rather than have my attorney do it. Just being at the courthouse again was traumatic. After spending so much time there over the past few months, my stomach began to knot as I walked from the parking deck to the courthouse steps. On top of everything today was a Monday. Now I know from experience that the two worst and busiest days to go to the courthouse for anything are Mondays and Fridays. I already wanted to vomit.

Once in the Clerk of Court office I found a spot at one of the public tables. I spread out all my documents and tried to make sense of what I was supposed to file at which window. All the legal ease was confusing and soon I was overwhelmed. The court clerks were short tempered and not much help. After an hour of trying to make sense of the paperwork I was so frustrated and angry that I began to cry.

These weren't the silent tears that quietly rolled down my cheeks for me to discreetly blot away with a tissue. No. This was the ugly cry. The meltdown cry. The one where I sounded like a pig snorting and gasping for air while wiping snot and tears with my sleeve, my shirt collar, even the hem of my shirt while fifty strangers looked on! The ugly cry.

I didn't want anybody to see me so I slumped to the floor hiding my head in my hands. I cried out loud "Please God! I don't know what to do. I have to have some help. Please just send me an angel! Please just send me an angel right now to help me file these papers."

As the words left my mouth, I could feel someone standing very near. Still hiding my face, I hoped whoever it was would just move on. When I lifted my head there was a young woman standing in front of me. She looked familiar, but I couldn't remember her name. Our eyes met. She seemed to recognize me too. Trying to fake a smile as I wiped my tears with the back of my hand and wished she would leave me to my pity party. Instead she said "Hey! We've met before, right?"

I said, "I think so. You look familiar. My name is Heather." I continued to blubber "Sorry I'm a mess. It's been... It's been a tough year."

She said, "I remember you now. We met at Christie's house in Hillsborough. I was with Ulysses. Now, tell me why are you crying? How can I help you?"

I remembered meeting her, but was embarrassed that I didn't recall her name. "I don't know if you can help me. I'm trying to file these papers. I don't know what I'm doing. They have to be filed by 5:00 PM and it's already 4:55 and..." I said.

She said, "Let me see if I can help. I have experience with that. I'm working at a law office downtown. We can figure it out."

I said, "Thank you! Please tell me your name. I'm sorry I can't remember."

She said, "my name is Angel."

My tears came fast again. I said, "You're kidding! You are literally an answer to my prayers! I prayed just now that God would send me an angel to help me get through this, and here you are!"

Angel just smiled. She collected my paperwork and helped me file them on time. I thanked her profusely as we parted on the courthouse steps. It's been almost a decade since that day. Our paths have never crossed again. You never know how prayers will be answered or how angels will show up. After that day I learned all I have to do is ask.

This Little Light of Mine

This light of mine, I'm gonna let it shine.
This light of mine, I'm gonna let it shine.
This light of mine, I'm gonna let it shine.
Let it shine, let it shine, let it shine!

Hide it under a bushel, No!
I'm gonna let it shine.
Hide it under a bushel, No!
I'm gonna let it shine.
Hide it under a bushel, No!
I'm gonna let it shine.
Let it shine, let it shine, let it shine!

"This Little Light of Mine" is a gospel song that became an anthem of the civil rights movement in the 1950s and 1960s. Often mistakenly believed to have been sung on plantations during slavery, it was originally written by Harry Dixon Loes around 1920 as a children's song.

Matthew 5:14–16 (NASB)
14 "You are the light of the world. A city set on a
hill cannot be hidden; 15 nor does anyone light a
lamp and put it under a basket, but on the lamp
stand, and it gives light to all who are in the
house. 16 "Let your light shine before men in such
a way that they may see your good works, and
glorify your Father who is in heaven.

CHAPTER 13

Homemade Protection Tools

Easy Shields Straight from Your Kitchen

Over the centuries, traditions turn into "old wives' tales." You may know this one: if you spill the salt, throw a pinch of it over your left shoulder to ward off bad luck. The cultures of many native peoples and ancient religions contain practices in which a tangible item or talisman is empowered with an prayer to offer protection or safety. Each day in our modern world, you do common sense things to stay safe from harm like locking your doors, wearing a seatbelt, blocking stalkers on social media. Likewise, these two simple exercises will focus your intention on keeping your shields up to maintain your light.

On-Ice Shield

Materials needed: Plastic water bottle, white paper, pencil, freezer

Fill a plastic water bottle or plastic sandwich bag with water. Fill only 60% to allow for expansion when it freezes. Use a pencil to write your full name and birth date on a small, white piece of paper. On the opposite side, write "Freeze all connection with [insert full name of person you wish to be shielded from]." Fold the paper to a smaller size and place it in the water bottle. Put the bottle in the back of your freezer. Repeat weekly as needed.

Coffee Grounds Shield

Materials needed: Approx. 8" x 8" piece of aluminum foil, freshly brewed coffee grounds, brown paper bag, pencil

If you're under intense negative, psychic assault from voodoo or dark magic, this method is extremely powerful. Place the freshly brewed coffee grounds on the aluminum foil. In pencil write on a small piece of brown paper bag your full name and birth date. On the opposite side, write the name of the person you seek protection from. Include "Protect me from [insert full name]. Do not see. Do not touch. Do not taste. Do not hear. Do not think. Do not smell." Place the paper note in the center of the coffee grounds. Fold the foil around the grounds to make a sealed, secure pouch. Put the pouch in the freezer. Repeat every other day as needed. For protection against multiple people, create individual pouches.

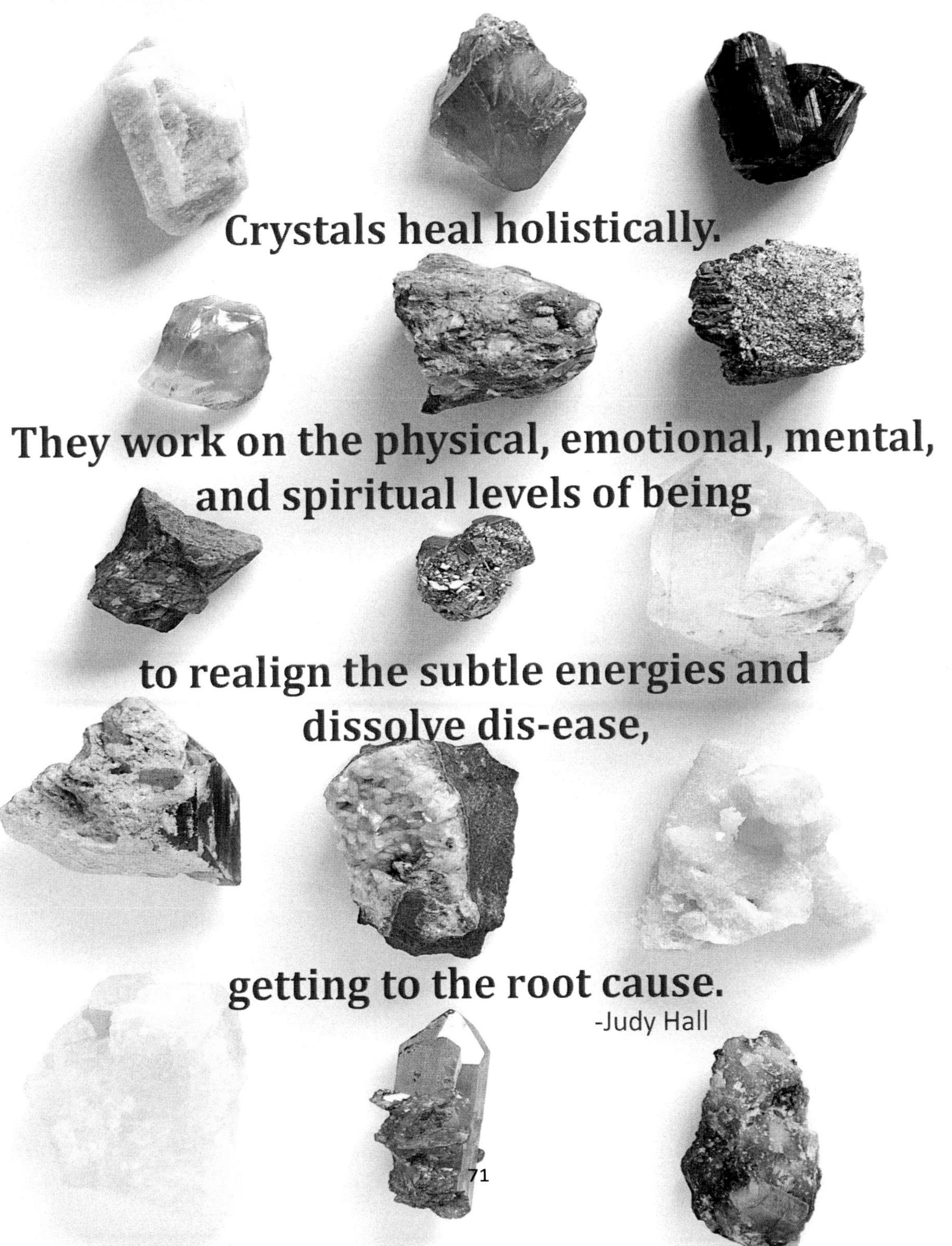
Crystals heal holistically.
They work on the physical, emotional, mental,
and spiritual levels of being
to realign the subtle energies and
dissolve dis-ease,
getting to the root cause.
-Judy Hall

CHAPTER 14

Crystals for Amplifying Your Light

Everyday Ways to Work with Crystals

Crystals and gemstones have been used by many civilizations over the centuries for their healing and energetic powers. Each crystal or stone has its own unique frequency and properties that promote healing and well-being. Crystals offer a gentle, non-invasive type of healing that supports your body's own repair systems to bring the body's systems back into balance. They work quickly to relieve minor ailments such as stomach ache or headache. More intense conditions can take longer to heal as they might be associated with an underlying disease or emotional dis-ease.

Crystal healing also helps you to uncover the psychosomatic or root causes of an ailment. Psychosomatic means the primary cause of the illness is developed in the mind. Crystal healing aligns with your thought patterns and beliefs, so if you believe in the process you will see results more rapidly. Some of the root causes of dis-ease are:

- Trauma, shock or attack
- Anxiety or fear
- Emotional exhaustion
- Damaged immune system
- Negative attitudes, emotions or stress

Where can I get crystals?

Just a few years ago you had to be a real rock hound to hunt for "rock shops" where you could buy crystals. Now you can get them at TJ Maxx, HomeGoods, and even Target! It's exciting how crystals have become semi-mainstream. If you don't have a rock shop in your town, you can always buy them online if you know what you're looking for. If not, it's best to visit a local metaphysical shop so you can touch the crystals and get a true feel for what you want and need. You can also get a sense of what certain crystals look like in raw form (page 71) versus smooth, tumbled versions (page 74). All rock shops have reference books for you to use and most stores have the crystals clearly marked and note their healing properties. While you're there be sure to ask the shop owner to tell you more about the crystals. They would love to help educate you!

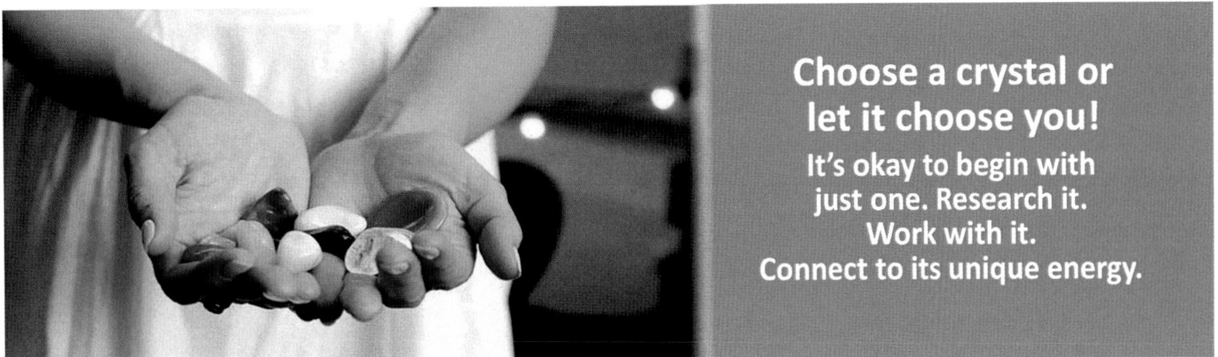

Choose a crystal or let it choose you!

With a little research you can determine which crystals are right for you. It's also fun to simply let your intuition guide you to the ones that feel right. Go to a shop that sells crystals and enjoy touching different stones. Are you attracted to the color, the shape, the texture? Which ones catch your eye and seem to say "Hey! Pick me up!" You will naturally be drawn to the crystal which has the properties your body or psyche needs to heal itself. Trust your gut! Choose a crystal that "feels good" to you. Look up more info on that stone - it's properties and uses. I guarantee you will be surprised and amazed that the stone your gut helps you select will be exactly what you need!

While in the shop, place the crystal you want to buy next to the description display. With your smartphone, take a photo them together and save it to a "Crystals" photo album on your phone for quick reference.

Resources for learning about crystals

There are so many resources and guides for learning about crystals. You can quickly type in the name of the stone and search for info on the Internet, which I do all the time. If you want a comprehensive guide to all things crystals, I feel the most excellent resource for beginners and experts alike is *The Crystal Bible: A Definitive Guide to Crystals Volumes 1, 2, and 3* by Judy Hall or *Crystal Healing* by Judy Hall.

How to use crystals

Crystals work best when worn against the skin. Wearing crystal jewelry - bracelets and necklaces - is an easy way to absorb their energy. You can tuck a smooth, tumbled crystal in your bra against your

HANDLE WITH CARE

Keep These Crystals Away from Sunlight

Some stones will fade in the sun. When they fade, so does the strength of their healing properties.

Amethyst Aquamarine Aventurine Beryl Citrine
Fluorite Kunzite Rose Quartz Sapphire Smokey Quartz

Crystals that Dissolve in Water

Angelite Ammolite Azurite Calcite
Celestite Fluorite Halite (Rock Salt)
Lepidolite Malachite Selenite Rhodochrosite

Salt Water Damages These Types of Crystals

Porous crystals Crystals that contain metal
Crystals that have water content (like Opal)
Pyrite Lapis Lazuli Hematite

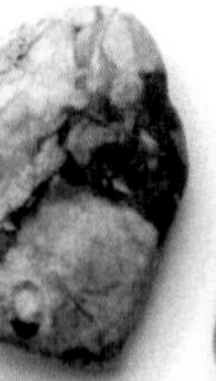
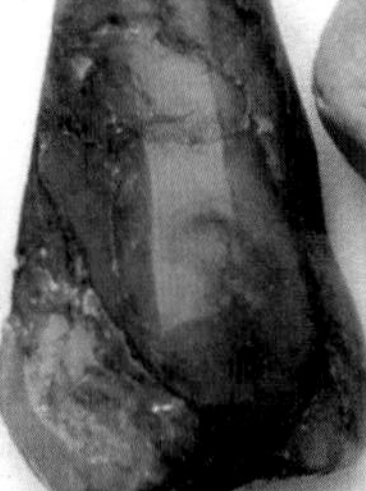

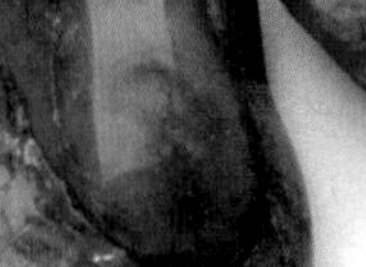

skin. Try putting a stone in your shirt or pants pocket, or carry a thumb stone (meditation stone). Adding a crystal to your drinking water is also a great way to absorb the healing properties of that stone. Shungite is a fabulous stone to put in your drinking water. It helps filter out harmful chemicals and balance your physical body. Place crystals on your desk or by your bed, under your bed, under your pillow, in your car, or anywhere you spend a lot of time and need an extra light boost. Add them to your bathwater and take a long soak. Be sure to note the list of crystals below that will dissolve in water!

Each crystal has a unique frequency and healing property. You can wear or carry as many different stones as you wish as they work well in combination and they are trendy and pretty!

Meditating with crystals

Placing crystals directly on your body is an easy way to assist with healing and balance. Lie down and place a crystal on your body over an area of pain, or underneath the body in that area. For mental or emotional stress, place a crystal between your eyebrows on your third eye. For a full chakra cleanse and balance lie down and place crystals on the corresponding chakras on your body as shown on page 81 - *The Super 7*. Rest and meditate for 30 minutes. Breathe deep into your belly and hold each breath to the count of seven before releasing. As you breathe in and hold, focus on the energy of each crystal as it transfers its energy into your body. When you feel balanced and recharged, take the crystals off your body starting from the crown (top of head) down to your feet. Be sure to clear them after use.

When to clear crystals

Crystals will work hard for you to absorb and transmute healing energies in your body and home. They should be cleared (or cleaned) on a regular basis to regain their effectiveness. When you buy new crystals or get them as a gift from someone, it's important to clear them to rid them of residual energy. Crystals need to be cleared:

- When other people have handled them.
- Frequently, and before and after they have been used for healing.
- After you buy them or get as a gift.
- After they have been in the presence of negative energies (arguments, chaos, heavy emotions, etc.).

Once your crystals have been cleared, they will begin recharging themselves using their own natural frequency of the earth.

How to clear crystals

Crystals are natural elements and gifts from the Earth. Using natural methods of clearing them is a safe and effective way to help them rest to their own natural frequencies. It's really easy to clear them by using one of the five elements: air, water, earth, fire, or metal.

Air: Pass the crystal through smoke from a fire, candle or any smudging tool like sage or incense, a campfire or fire pit too!

Water: Place them under cold water and let them air dry. (Be sure to note the list of stones on page 74 that will dissolve in water.) Dip them in a body of freshwater (pond, stream, lake, river) or in the ocean.

Earth: Crystals come from the earth so giving them a dirt bath is always a good way to help them recharge. You can bury them in the yard or simply put them in a container of potting soil or dirt. Your plants will appreciate the energy boost! Sea Salt is a great cleanser too. Pour sea salt into a glass or bowl and submerge your crystals in it for 24 hours.

Fire: You can put your crystals out in the sunlight, or moonlight for 24 hours to recharge. Each month during the full moon, I like to put all my crystals and the jewelry I wear most often out in the moonlight. I arrange them on a wooden serving tray, or use a cookie sheet if I don't have anything else. Put them outside at dusk and collect them the next morning.

Metal: Sound is a super way to recalibrate crystals to their optimal frequency. A few sound tools you can use are a cymbal, gong, drum, singing bowl, or tuning forks.

Don't forget to include your crystal jewelry! It's working hard for you too. Try different methods and see which one resonates with you. The monthly ritual can be fun and relaxing.

Top 7 Must-Have Crystals

There are seven key crystals you need in your lightworker toolbox to help align your chakras and amplify your light. Each of these seven powerhouse crystals have healing properties that connect with a specific chakra to help you regain balance physically and emotionally so your light can shine.

Red Jasper ***"Stone of Protection"***
Root Chakra | 1st Chakra | Red

- Red Jasper releases fear and negativity. It helps you deal with conflict and grounds your energy. Red Jasper represented fertility to Ancient Egyptians and symbolized the blood of Mother Earth to Native Americans.
- Red Jasper helps balance the Root Chakra, located at the base of the spine. This chakra relates to issues of physical security, survival, and basic material needs.
- Balanced Root Chakra: a sense of one's own power, independent, spontaneous leadership, feeling of abundance, safety,  security, self assured, confident, at ease.
- Unbalanced Root Chakra: impatient, hyperactive, highly impulsive, angry, manipulative, fear or worry about money, career, home, security, physical needs met, obsessing about money, possessions, a workaholic mindset

Carnelian ***"Stone of Courage/ Creativity"***
Sacral Chakra | 2nd Chakra | Orange

- Carnelian helps you focus and harness your energy for success, to have courage, removes self doubt, helps you be decisive, independent, self-aware and creative.
- Carnelian balances the Sacral Chakra, located below the naval, midway to the base of the spine. This chakra relates to issues with body image, procreation, creativity, physical desires, appetites, addictions, sexuality, and courage.
- Balanced Sacral Chakra: courageous, fertile, confident, joyful, sexually confident, creative.

- Unbalanced Sacral Chakra: low self-esteem, infertility, sluggish, fear or worry about body image, fertility, sex

Citrine ***"Stone of Success"***
Solar Plexus Chakra / 3rd Chakra / Yellow

- Citrine is said to carry the energy of the sun, so it brings joy, warmth and confidence. It is a stone of joyful communication and teaches you how to manage your money and joyfully give and receive. It helps you overcome fears and phobias.
- Citrine helps balance the Solar Plexus Chakra, located just above the naval. You may feel this chakra when you are anxious and have a spasm in your diaphragm.
- Balanced Sacral Chakra: relates to power and control, emotional connections, empathy, good energy, logical, organized, intelligent
- Unbalanced Solar Plexus: lazy, overly emotional, cynical, energy leach, fear or worry about gaining control or losing your power.

Green Aventurine ***"Stone of Luck"***
Heart Chakra / 4th Chakra / Light Green

- Aids in manifesting prosperity, wealth. Attracts abundance and good fortune. Used as a healer of the heart, both physically and emotionally, especially useful after a breakup. It helps ease panic attacks and calms emotions. Green Aventurine works with the Heart Chakra, located in the center of the chest. This chakra relates to love & relationships.
- Balanced Heart Chakra: loving, generous, compassionate, nurturing, accepting, positive self love, joyful, buoyant
- Unbalanced Heart Chakra: unloving, unable to show love, jealous, insecure, possessive, fear or worry about giving or receiving love, obsessing about a relationship

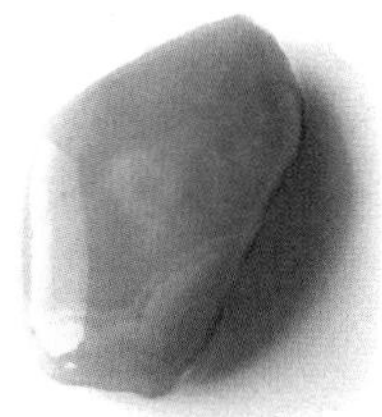

Blue Lace Agate *"Stone of Peace"*
Throat Chakra | 5th Chakra | Light Blue

- Blue Lace Agate enables you to communicate clearly and speak your truth. It relieves mental stress, dissolves anger, helps to develop your intuition and clairvoyance.
- Blue Lace Agate works with the Throat Chakra, located in the throat just below the Adam's Apple. This chakra relates to clear communication.
- Balanced Throat Chakra: able to speak your truth, receptive, loyal, decisive, and clear with your intentions.
- Unbalanced Throat Chakra: unable to speak your truth, dogmatic, disloyal, fear of being condemned or punished for beliefs that differ from those of your family or peer group, obsessing about a relationship.

Sodalite *"Stone of Wisdom"*
3rd Eye Chakra | 6th Chakra | Dark Blue

- Sodalite helps you make wise decisions and gently opens your 3rd eye or inner knowing. It allows you to receive spiritual messages and guidance and helps release your shadow side.
- Sodalite works with the 3rd Eye Chakra, located in the center of forehead in the brow between the eyes. This chakra, also known as the brow chakra, relates to intuition, seeing the future.
- Balanced 3rd Eye Chakra: intuitive, perceptive, visionary, sees clearly the past, present and future, hopeful, insightful, open-minded.
- Unbalanced 3rd Eye: fearful, angry, spiteful, superstitious, overly concerned with other people's thoughts, fear or worry about the past, present or future, inability to plan or set goals, difficulty concentrating, tendency to space out, nightmares

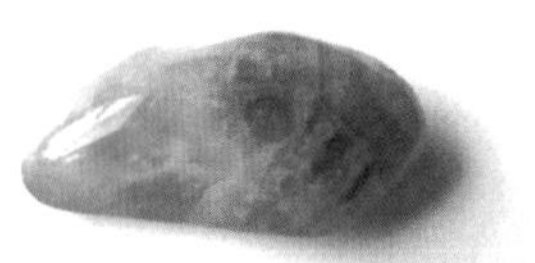

Amethyst *"A Stone Spirituality"*
Crown Chakra / 7th Chakra / Purple

- Amethyst is an extremely powerful crystal for both healing and protection. It enables you to reach higher levels of thinking, assists us in overcoming addictions of any kind, combats anger, rage, fear, impatience and restlessness. It helps you open your mind to higher realms of spiritual understanding.
- Amethyst supports the Crown Chakra, located on the top of your skull. This chakra deals with spiritual, divine knowing, clear thinking, claircognizance.
- Balanced Crown Chakra: mystical, creative, humanitarian, connected to the Divine, helps you make decisions, increases selflessness, helps to focus your thoughts on higher, more spiritual pursuits.
- Unbalanced Crown Chakra: arrogant, overly imaginative, uses power to control others, fear or worry about separation & isolation, lack of belief in a higher power or God, boastful, spiritual addictions, overly concerned with humanity and material concerns.

Crystals and kids

Have you noticed children love stones and crystals? They really do! Kids have a natural connection to the earth so they are innately drawn to crystals and their healing properties. Children may be even more receptive to their healing powers because they intuitively select the crystal that interests them and do not have preconceived judgments about "playing with rocks." Crystals can help kids to focus, manage their energy and emotions, feel safe and protected, reduce feelings of inadequacy or separation anxiety, and sleep better. They are relatively inexpensive and make great gifts!

THE SUPER 7

Powerhouse, Must-Have Crystals for your Toolbox

There are seven key crystals you need in your lightworker toolbox to help align and shine! Each of these seven powerhouse crystals have healing properties that connect with a specific chakra to help you regain physical and emotional balance.

Red Jasper	Carnellian	Citrine	Green Aventurine	Blue Lace Agate	Sodalite	Amethyst
Stone of Protection	Stone of Courage & Creativity	Stone of Success	Stone of Luck	Stone of Peace	Stone of Wisdom	Stone of Spirituality
Root Chakra	Sacral Chakra	Solar Plexus	Heart Chakra	Throat Chakra	3rd Eye Chakra	Crown Chakra
Releases fear and negativity. Promotes safety, security, abundance	Removes self-doubt. Promotes creativity, independence, courage, energy	Releases phobias and worry. Promotes joy, confidence, organization	Removes heartache. Promotes love, compassion, empathy, kindness	Removes dogma. Promotes peaceful discussions, clear intentions	Removes confusion. Promotes intuition, open-mindedness, tranquillity	Releases control issues. Promotes selflessness, spiritual understanding

Note: Two other super stones to add to your collection are Rose Quartz and Crystal Quartz. Rose Quartz supports the heart chakra and Crystal Quartz supports all the chakras and works in tandem to amplify the crystals shown above.

CHAPTER 15

Essential Oils

Bringing Balance & Light to Mind, Body, and Spirit

Essential oils are powerful healers that can assist in recognizing trapped emotions and releasing them from our chakras. Some essential oils are considered more than 50 times more potent than dried herbs. Used topically, aromatically, or internally, oils can help to balance your chakras and raise your vibration which will aid in healing many emotional and physical issues of dis-ease. Oils like frankincense, sage, lavender and lemon can also be used to ward off negative energy and increase mental focus. Individual essential oils or oil blends can help to bring the body and mind back into balance - and they smell great too!

How to use essential oils

Pure essential oils used in appropriate amounts are absolutely safe for your and your family. Make sure to select high-quality essential oils that go through extensive purity testing to ensure safety. Read the label! If the label has a warning such as "do not use on small children, do not ingest, do not use if pregnant." Then you should not use that oil at all! Your skin is your largest organ. Applying an oil topically (on the skin) is the same as ingesting it. So if there is a warning that says the oil is not safe to put *in* your body, it is not safe to put it *on* your body either.

Aromatically: Simply smell the oil from the bottle or place a few drops in the palms of your hands. Rub hands together and inhale deeply for 1 to 3 minutes. Place a few drops in an oil diffuser to dispense the aroma into the air to get the healing benefits of that oil.

Topically: Place 1-2 drops of essential oil into the palm of hand and apply to areas of discomfort or chakra. *Note: If you are using an essential oil that may be irritating to the skin, use a natural carrier oil to dilute it.* Natural carrier oils can include: coconut oil, almond oil, grape seed oil, jojoba, olive oil, sunflower oil or other oils that do not control petroleum such as baby oil. If you are using more than one oil, or layering, allow a few minutes between application for each oil to absorb into the skin.

Internally: Most essential oils can be

Single Oils to Help Balance Your Chakras

Crown Chakra:	**Frankincense, Vetiver, Sandalwood, Spruce**
Third Eye Chakra:	**Lemon, Rosemary, Basil, Clary Sage**
Throat Chakra:	**Lavender, Roman Chamomile, Birch**
Heart Chakra:	**Lime, Thyme, Jasmine, Geranium, Ylang Ylang**
Solar Plexus:	**Lemon, Ginger, Bergamot, Clove, Fennel**
Sacral Chakra:	**Wild Orange, Ylang-ylang, Cinnamon, Neroli**
Root Chakra:	**Arborvitae, Patchouli, Cedarwood, Myrrh**

taken internally, but carefully check all safety information and warning labels first. Wintergreen should not be ingested.

Essential oil safety

Consult an expert if you have questions about the safe use of essential oils. Always supervise children when using oils. Children and elders have delicate skin, so it's recommended to dilute oils before applying them topically as noted above. It's best to apply oil to the bottom of a child's feet before you try other areas. Avoid putting oils into the nose, inner ears, eyes, broken skin or other sensitive areas. Research which oils may pose a risk for sun and skin sensitivity and, as with any medicine, always exercise caution and always read the labels.

Essential oil blends

Essential oils can be used individually or combined for a more potent emotional and physical effect. There is no right or wrong combination of oils. Use what you have, use what you like, or research the properties of each oil to mix them together for your desired result. Thankfully, essential oils are really popular now, so you can search online for roller bottle blend recipes or find many books on the topic. You can create roller bottles or put them in other glass containers. It's important to use glass or metal containers; essential oils react with plastic and erode it. Shop online for glass bottles in sizes less than 1/4 oz. or for 10 ml roller bottles. These containers work perfectly for small batches. Fill half your bottle with the essential oils and top off the other half with the carrier oil. It's that simple!

You will also need a natural carrier oil to make your blends. Carrier oils are made from plants and are used to dilute essential oils and "carry" them to your skin. This means it makes the essential oils spread farther on your skin. Essential oils are potent and some of them can cause irritation when applied directly to your skin.

Most carrier oils are unscented or lightly scented and do not interfere with an essential oil's therapeutic properties. Carrier oils may be used alone or with other oils to nourish your skin. A popular carrier oil is fractionated coconut oil because it doesn't have a scent. Other common carrier oils are:

- almond oil,
- grape seed oil,
- jojoba oil,
- avocado oil,
- sunflower oil,
- olive oil.

Chakras Balance Roller Bottle Blends

Essential oils are amazing, natural tools for your lightworker toolbox. If you're a regular oil user, you'll know just how potent and powerful they can be. Roller bottles are really handy. It's easy to make your blends in advance and have them on hand rather than layering single oils on the skin. Roller blends can be easily to be applied to the wrists, neck, belly, feet, and over the chakras.

Once you have selected the essential oils you would like to use in your blend, you will need to select a carrier oil. Carrier oils dilute the essential oil to act as a base and "carries" the essential oil that is being mixed with it. This helps your essential oil cover more surface area, and better penetrate the surface of the skin for added benefits. Carrier oils do not evaporate quickly like essential oils do. Essential oils can cause sensitivity when applied undiluted directly to the skin. The carrier oil helps to eliminate skin sensitivity.

I recommend using fractionated coconut oil as a carrier because it is odorless and fast-absorbing. You can also use any natural oil such as grape seed, almond oil, sunflower seed oil, etc. Do not use baby oil. Baby oil is petroleum based and will react negatively with the essential oils.

How to make a roller bottle

- Start with a 10 ml glass roller bottle. You can buy then online in packs of 5 or in bulk.
- Add the drops of essential oil. See my favorite roller bottle blend recipes shown here!
- Fill the rest of 10 ml roller bottles with a carrier oil of your choice.
- Snap on the roller ball. Make sure to press it down firmly to the glass bottle rim.
- Shake the bottle to mix the carrier oil and essential oils.
- Apply over the chakra noted with each blend or roll on the wrists, neck, feet, or belly.

"Amazing Grace"
Crown Chakra
10 Frankincense
10 Sandalwood
12 Lavender
6 Rosemary

"Crystal Visions"
3rd Eye Chakra
10 Frankincense
10 Lemongrass
8 Clary Sage
8 Lavender

"Speak Up"
Throat Chakra
10 Lavender
10 Lime
8 Cypress
6 Peppermint

"Heart and Soul"
Heart Chakra
10 Geranium
8 Peppermint
8 Grapefruit
6 Marjoram

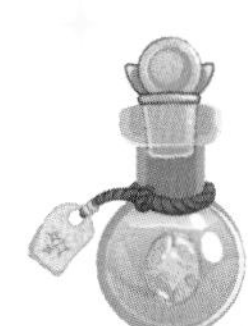

"I've got this!"
Solar Plexus Chakra
10 Bergamot
10 Grapefruit
10 Ginger
8 Lemon

"Let it Go"
Sacral Chakra
10 Wild Orange
10 Lemon
8 Peppermint
8 Tangerine

"Safe & Secure"
Root Chakra
10 Arborvitae
10 Cinnamon
8 Cedarwood
6 Cinnamon

CHAPTER 16

How to See in the Dark

The Root Cause of Your Power Outage

You've burned all the sage. You're wearing all the crystals. You've spoken aloud your intentions until your throat is raw. You've unhooked from negative people, so why is your light still dim? It may be necessary for you to learn to see in the dark. All the healing arts tips and tools will not work for long if there is a deeper issue at the root of the problem. The root cause is often within us, not a projection from outside people or forces. Over and over again our deep-rooted fears and lack of self-worth will extinguish any light we hope to ignite until we really look at the truth of the situation.

Do you continually attract toxic people, narcissists, and energy vampires? Are you stressed about body image, financial stability, guilt, or unbalanced relationships? Do you feel out of control? Healing arts tools can help eliminate these issues; but first, it is absolutely necessary to do your "inner work." Perhaps you attract toxic people because you have codependent tendencies. Maybe you feel out of control and "attacked" because you have repeatedly given away your power. In our modern society of quick fixes and instant gratification, it's become too easy for us to grab onto the next rapid results tool to change our outer issues rather than work on the inner ones. Self-awareness, growth, and personal development are crucial to igniting and maintaining your light. You have to do the inner work.

Substance abuse, negative self-talk, anger, depression, fear, anxiety are all conditions that lower your life force and keep you in the dark. Lower energies, whether in human or spirit form, prey on your fears and low mood. In order for you to shine, it is crucial that you do your own inner work to transform your blocked emotions, fears, and insecurities.

Sometimes you can't see the root causes of your own patterns and issues, you only know that you're stuck. It's always a great idea to seek counseling from a qualified therapist. They can help you determine behaviors that keep you in a constant spin and provide the plan and tools to help you move forward. Group therapy or spiritual mentoring are also effective to help you shift out of your own stuck spaces. Alternative healing modalities like Reiki, acupuncture, cranial-sacral, or kundalini yoga can also be very helpful and work in tandem with traditional therapy.

Taking back your light is not always easy, but it is always worth the work. It will involve being your authentic self, which can be difficult. You must bring the root issues to the surface so you can heal them. This may involve extreme self care and establishing firm emotional and physical boundaries. Crystals and oils and other healing arts tools can support you, but you have to boldly guard your light in order to shine. You can do it! Now you have to tools to shine so brightly! You are ready to see into the dark and take back your light!

It's okay
if you fall down
and lose
your spark.
Just make sure
when you
get back up,
you rise as
the whole
damn
fire.
- Collette Werden

Bibliography

With gratitude to all my great teachers and mentors.
Thank you for shining the light!

Askinosie, Heather and Jandro, Timmi. Crystal Maus: Everyday Rituals To Tune In To The Real You. Hay House, Inc. 2017.

Barhum, Lana. "What are the Benefits of an Epsom Salt Detox?"Medical News Today, 26 April 2018, www.medicalnewstoday.com/articles/321627#benefits-of-epsom-salt-baths

Bowen, Deb, and Fey, Samatha. Psychic Teachers Podcast. 2010-2020.

Cameron, Julia. The Artist's Way®: A Spiritual Path to Higher Creativity. Penguin/Putnam, Inc. ©1992, 2002.

Caputo, Tara. Personal Interview. 2020. www.psychictara.com

Connolly, David. In Search of Angels. Perigee Books©1993

"*Crystal Properties & Uses Clear Quartz.*" Psychic Revelation. www.psychic-revelation.com/reference/a_d/crystals/quartz_clear.html

Davis, Faith. "*Everything Your Need to Know About Cleating and Charging Crystals.*" Cosmic Cuts. 2018. cosmiccuts.com/blogs/healing-stones-blog/clearing-and-charging-crystals

doTERRA® International Conference. Salt Lake City, Utah. September 2014, 2015.

Fey, Samantha. samanthafey.com

Graham, Billy. Angels. Word Publishing. ©1975, 1986, 1995.

Hall, Judy. Crystals for Healing. Octopus Publishing Group. ©2005, 2011.

Hall, Judy. The Crystal Bible: A Definitive Guide To Crystals. Godsfield Press, Ltd. 2003.
Hay, Louise. Heal Your Body: The Mental Causes for Physical Illness and the Metaphysical Way to Overcome Them. Hay House, Inc. ©1982, 1984.

Hay, Louise. You Can Heal Your Life®. Hay House, Inc. ©1984, 1987, 2004.

Jessup, Verdell. The 3 Types of Entities (and How to Know if You Have One) verdelljessup.com

The Holy Bible King James Version. Thomas Nelson Publishers, Inc. 1989.

Emotions & Essential Oils: A Modern Resource for Healing, Emotional Reference Guide. Third Edition. Enlighten, Alternative Healing, LLC. Revised Fall 2014.

Kondō, Marie. The Life-Changing Magic of Tidying Up: The Japanese Art of Decluttering and Organizing. 2014.

Lancer, Darlene, JD, MFT. "The Price and Payoff of a Gray Rock Strategy." Psychology Today. 4 Nov, 2019 www.psychologytoday.com/us/blog/toxic-relationships/201911/the-price-and-payoff-gray-rock-strategy.

Lozanova, Sarah. "5 Tips to Safeguard Against Electromagnetic Radiation." Earth 911. 28 August, 2019. https://earth911.com/eco-tech/electromagnetic-radiation-safeguards.

Lucas, Jim. "*What Is Electromagnetic Radiation?*" Live Science. 13 March, 2015. www.livescience.com/38169-electromagnetism.html

Modern Essentials, A Contemporary Guide to the Therapeutic Use of Essential Oils, 7th Edition. AromaTools ISBN 978-1-937702-39-7. 2015.

Pall, Martin L. "*Wi-Fi is an Important Threat to Human Health.*" Science Direct. July 2018. www.sciencedirect.com/science/article/pii/S0013935118300355

Rand, William Lee. Registered Holy Fire® III Karuna Reiki® Master Training Manual. The International Center for Reiki Training ©William L. Rand. 1995-2019.

Richardson, Kerri. What Your Clutter Is Trying to Tell You: Uncover the Message in the Mess and Reclaim Your Life. © 2017

Shapiro, Ed and Deb. The Unexpected Power of Mindfulness & Meditation. ©2017.

Shirer, Priscilla. The Armor of God - Bible Study Book. Adult Ministry Publishing. LifeWay Church Resources. 2015.

Smith, Linda. Called Into Healing: Reclaiming Our Judeo-Christian Legacy of Healing Touch, 2nd Edition. 2006.

Spriggs, Gina. Smudging FAQs. GinaSpriggs.Guru

Truman, Boyd K. Symphony of the Cells® Training Conference. Charlotte, NC. September 2017.

Truman, Karol Kuhn. Feelings Buried Alive Never Die. ©1991, 2003.

Van der Kolk, Bessel, M.D. The Body Keeps the Score: Brain, Mind, and Body in the Healing of Trauma, 2014.

Virtue, Doreen. Angels 101: An Introduction to Connecting, Working, and Healing with the Angels. Hay House, Inc. 2006.

Virtue, Doreen. Archangels 101 : How to Connect Closely with Archangels Michael, Raphael, Uriel, Gabriel and Others for Healing, Protection, and Guidance. Hay House, Inc. ©2011

Virtue, Doreen. How to Hear your Angels. Hay House, Inc. ©2007.

Winkowski, Mary Ann. When Ghosts Speak: Understanding the World of Earthbound Spirits. 2007.

Photography Credits

Page	Description Photo Credit
Cover	Take Back Your Light. Luizclas from Pexels
1	Woman lights . Oleg-Magni from Pexels
2	Chakra female. Dmytro Flisak. Shutterstock
3	Sunflowers. Andre Furtado from Pexels
5	Girl. Melissa Askew from Unsplash
6	Bath. Hisu-lee-2qvxIr_DXGo from Unsplash
7	Star night. Egil Sjøholt from Pexels
10	Rainbow Road. Tony Ross from Unsplash
12	Girl phone. Egil Sjøholt from Pexels
13	Salt lamp. Marcos Paulo Prado from Unsplash
14	Computers. Andreas palmer from Unsplash
15	Incense. Denis-oliveira from Unsplash
16	FemSkyline. Jeffery Erhunse from Unsplash
17	Sage and Shell. Heather Robinson
18	Tools. CoralAntlerCreative. Shuttertock
19	Girl sage. Brittany-colette from Unsplash
21	Sage bundle. Marcos Paulo Prado. Unsplash
22	Florida Water. Heather Robinson
22	Sea Salt . Maria Petersson from Pexels
24	Himalayan salt. Monicore from Pexels
24	White sea salt. Alex from Pexles
25	Free-to-use-sounds XtQNZRTIMYc / Unsplash
26	Wind chimes. Lavi Perchiki from Unsplash
27	Protection stones. Heather Robinson
33	Essential vial. Sarah Gualtieri from Unsplash
35	Lightbulb. Luca Nardone from Pexels
38	Girl branches. Joseph Gonzalez from Unsplash
40	Woman bubble. Shutterstock 70577773
41	Lantern. Gantas Vaičiulėnas from Pexels
42	Shield. Paweł Czerwiński from Unsplash
43	Peace candle. Ai Nhan from Unsplash
44	Gray rocks. Jessica Johnston from Unsplash
48	Watercolor people. Shutterstock_713857579
49	Cords. David Waschbüsch from Pexels
50	Tulips. Marta Teron from Shutterstock
51	Sad woman B&W. Kat Jayne from Pexels
52	Paper robot.Burak Kostak from Pexels
52	Hooks. Shutterstock
54	Bracelets. Heather Robinson
55	Sleep. Cottonbro from Pexels
58	Quartz. Dani Costelo from Unsplash
59	Crystal line art,Shutterstock_1045315381
59-50	Protection stones. Heather Robinson
61	Crystals outside. Heather Robinson
64	Angel headphones. Maisei Raman.Shutterstock
67	Angel Illustration, Shutterstock_1320030413
69	Candle. Moodywalk from Unsplash.
71	Raw crystals. Franco Antonio Giovanella from Unsplash
73	Hands crystals. Sara Johnston from Pexels
74	Crystal circle. Franco Antonio Giovanella from Unsplash
77-80	Individual stones. Heather Robinson
80	Mom & Child chakra. Shutterstock_1312664387
81	Super 7. Nikki Zalewski from Shutterstock
83	Applying oil. Chelsea Shapouri from Unsplash
86	Bottles. Illustration: Salenta from Shutterstock
87	Man sparkler. Warren Wong from Unsplash
87	Man beach. Mohamed Nohassi from Unsplash
89	Fire eater. Marko from Unsplash

About The Author

Heather Robinson is a lightworker and holistic healer. She is a Usui/Holy Fire® III Karuna® Reiki Master practitioner with a passion for teaching and sharing her accumulated knowledge of healing arts to help others.

 @heatherrobinsonhealingarts

 @heatherhealingarts

HeatherHealingArts.com

Made in the USA
Columbia, SC
20 April 2022